easy knitting
Weekend

easy knitting
Weekend

30 quick projects to make for your home and to wear

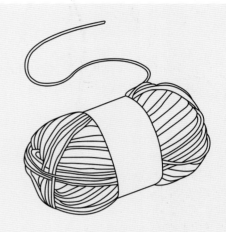

Consultant: Nikki Trench

hamlyn

An Hachette UK Company
www.hachette.co.uk

First published in Great Britain in 2013 by
Hamlyn, a division of Octopus Publishing Group Ltd
Endeavour House
189 Shaftesbury Avenue
London
WC2H 8JY
www.octopusbooks.co.uk

ISBN 978-0-600-62831-6

A CIP catalogue record for this book is available from the
British Library

Printed and bound in China

10 9 8 7 6 5 4 3 2 1

Contents

Introduction

If you can knit a few basic stitches, you can create stylish knitted items to wear, use to decorate your home and give as gifts for friends and family.

Whether you are a relative beginner, a confident convert or a long-term aficionado, there are projects here to delight. While your first attempts may be a bit uneven, a little practice and experimentation will ensure you soon improve. None of the projects here is beyond the scope of even those fairly new to the hobby.

It is always satisfying to create something from scratch, and even more so when achieved quickly. All the projects here, which range from stylish items to wear – a beret, scarves and slippers – through to practical accessories such as phone covers and a doorstop, can be completed quickly, even over a weekend. All would make good gifts.

Knitting essentials
All you really need to get knitting is a pair of needles and some yarn. For some projects, that's it; for others additional items are required, most of which can be found in a fairly basic sewing kit. All measurements are given in metric and imperial. Choose which to work in and stick with it since conversions may not be exact.
- **Needles** These come in metric (mm), British and US sizes and are made from different materials, all of which affect the weight and 'feel' of the needles – which you choose is down to personal preference. Circular and double-pointed needles are sometimes used as well.
- **Yarns** Specific yarns are listed for each project, but full details of the yarn's composition and the ball lengths are given so that you can choose alternatives, either from online sources or from your local supplier, many of whom have very knowledgeable staff. Do keep any leftover yarns (not forgetting the ball bands, since these contain vital information) to use for future projects.
- **Additional items**: Some projects require making up and finishing, and need further materials or equipment, such as sewing needles, buttons and other accessories. These are detailed in each project's Getting Started box.

What is in this book
All projects are illustrated with several photographs to show you the detail of the work – both inspirational and useful for reference. A full summary of each project is given in the Getting Started box so you can see exactly what's involved. Here, projects are graded from one ball of yarn (straightforward, suitable for beginners) through two (more challenging) to three balls (for knitters with more confidence and experience).

Also in the Getting Started box is the size of each finished item, yarn(s), needles and additional items needed, and what tension/gauge the project is worked in. Finally, a breakdown of the steps involved is given so you know exactly what the project entails before you start.

At the beginning of the pattern instructions is a key to all abbreviations that are used in that project, while occasional notes expand on the pattern instructions where necessary.

If you have enjoyed the projects here, you may want to explore the other titles in the Easy Knitting series: *Babies & Children, Chic, Cosy, Country* and *Vintage & Retro*. For those who enjoy crochet, a sister series, Easy Crochet, features similarly stylish yet simple projects.

Metric	British	US
2 mm	14	0
2.5 mm	13	1
2.75 mm	12	2
3mm	11	n/a
3.25 mm	10	3
3.5 mm	n/a	4
3.75 mm	9	5
4 mm	8	6
4.5 mm	7	7
5 mm	6	8
5.5 mm	5	9
6 mm	4	10
6.5 mm	3	10.5
7 mm	2	n/a
7.5 mm	1	n/a
8 mm	0	11
9 mm	0	13
10 mm	0	15

Colourful cushions

Once you get started, you'll find yourself creating a production line of different colours, styles and patterns.

GETTING STARTED

 Straightforward items with no shaping, so quick to make

Size:

Dark blue garter stitch: 50cm x 50cm (20in x 20in),
Orange rib: 40cm x 40cm (16in x 16in), **Green**
moss/seed stitch: *40cm x 40cm (16in x 16in),* **Yellow**
ochre and pale blue garter stitch: *30cm x 30cm*
(12in x 12in)

How much yarn:

Dark blue garter stitch: 8 x 50g (2oz) balls Debbie Bliss Cashmerino Aran, approx 90m (98 yards) per ball; 1 x 50g (2oz) ball contrasting colour

Orange rib: 5 x 50g (2oz) balls Debbie Bliss Cashmerino Aran

Green moss/seed stitch: 5 x 50g (2oz) balls Debbie Bliss Cashmerino Aran

Yellow ochre garter stitch: 7 x 50g (2oz) balls Debbie Bliss Cashmerino Chunky, approx 65m (79 yards) per ball

Pale blue garter stitch: 3 x 50g (2oz) balls Debbie Bliss Cashmerino Aran

Needles:

Pair of 5mm (no. 6/US 8) needles for all cushions/ pillows except yellow ochre garter stitch which uses pair of 7mm (no. 2/US 10½) needles

Additional items:

Buttons to finish if required
Cushion pads/pillow forms

Tension/gauge:

Garter stitch – 18 stitches and 40 rows to 10cm (4in) on 5mm (no. 6/US 8) needles and using Debbie Bliss Cashmerino Aran OR 14 stitches and 32 rows to 10cm (4in) on 7mm (no. 2/US 10½) needles using Cashmerino Chunky

Moss/seed stitch – 18 stitches and 32 rows to 10cm (4in) on 5mm (no. 6/US 8)) needles using Debbie Bliss Cashmerino Aran

Rib pattern – 15 stitches and 24 rows to 10cm on 5mm (no. 6/US 8)) needles using Debbie Bliss Cashmerino Aran

What you have to do:

Cast on. Knit in garter stitch, moss/seed stitch or rib pattern. Make simple button holes if required. Cast/bind off.

This selection of cushions/pillows includes garter stitch, rib stitch and moss/seed stitch versions. You can mix and match or stick to one style in different sizes and colours.

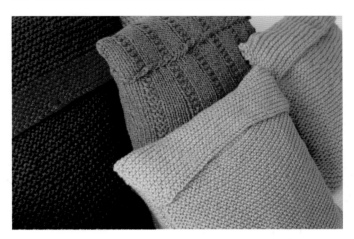

The Yarn

We have used Debbie Bliss Cashmerino Aran for all the cushions/pillows except the yellow ochre one, which is knitted in Cashmerino Chunky. Both these yarns are a soft mixture of 12% cashmere, 55% merino wool and 33% microfibre and come in a wonderful range of colours. Go for bright primary shades as shown here, or choose a more subdued pastel palette.

Abbreviations:
cm = centimetre(s);
g st = garter stitch (every row knit);
st(s) = stitch(es);
WS = wrong side

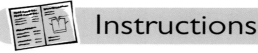

Instructions

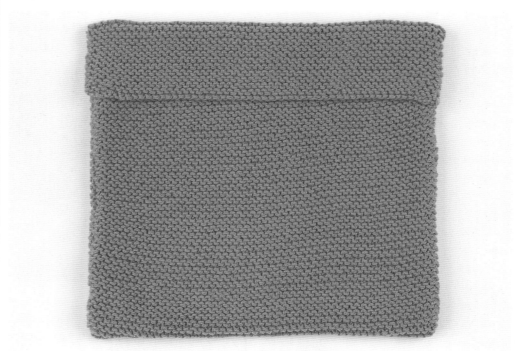

GARTER STITCH:
Dark blue cushion/pillow:

Using 5mm (no.6/US 8) needles and dark blue yarn cast on 90 sts.

Knit every row to form garter stitch (g st) until the work measures 100cm (40in).

Do not join the yarn mid-row when you need to change to a new ball, but finish the old ball at the end of a row and then work on the new ball for the next row. You can knit the first 2 stitches with both yarns to join in the new ball. Change to contrasting yarn and knit 24 more rows.

Next row: Knit 6 stitches, (cast/bind off 3 stitches, knit 12 stitches), repeat to last 9 stitches; cast/bind off 3 stitches, knit 6 stitches.

Next row: Knit 6 stitches (cast on 3 stitches, knit 12), repeat to last 6 stitches; cast on 3 stitches, knit 6 stitches. The last 2 rows form the buttonholes.

Knit 2 more rows.

Cast/bind off knitwise.

Yellow ochre cushion/pillow:

Using 7mm (no.2/10½in) needles cast on 43 sts.

Knit every row to form garter stitch (g st) until the work measures 65cm (25½in).

Do not join the yarn mid-row when you need to change to a new ball, but finish the old ball at the end of a row and then work on the new ball for the next row. You can knit the first 2 stitches with both yarns to join in the new ball. Cast/bind off knitwise.

Pale blue cushion/pillow:

Using 5mm (no.6/US 8) needles cast on 55 sts.

Knit every row to form garter stitch (g st) until the work measures 65cm (25½in).

Do not join the yarn mid-row when you need to change to a new ball, but finish the old ball at the end of a row and then work on the new ball for the next row. You can knit the first 2 stitches with both yarns to join in the new ball.

Cast/bind off knitwise.

RIB PATTERN:
Orange cushion/pillow:

Using 5mm (no.6/US 8) needles cast on 61 sts.

1st row: (RS) Knit 5, *purl 3, knit 5, repeat from * to end.

2nd row: (WS) Purl to end.

These two rows form the rib pattern and are repeated to the end of the work.

Continue in rib pattern until the work measures 86cm (34in), ending with a purl row.

Do not join the yarn mid-row when you need to change

to a new ball, but finish the old ball at the end of a row and then work on the new ball for the next row. You can knit the first 2 stitches with both yarns to join in the new ball. Cast/bind off.

MOSS/SEED STITCH:
Green cushion/pillow:

Using 5mm (no.6/US 8) needles cast on 73 sts.
1st row: (RS) Knit 1, (purl 1, knit 1) to end.
This single row forms the moss/seed stitch pattern and is repeated for every row.
Continue in moss/seed stitch until the work measures 86cm (34in).
Do not join the yarn mid-row when you need to change to a new ball, but finish the old ball at the end of a row and then work on the new ball for the next row. You can knit the first 2 stitches with both yarns to join in the new ball. Cast/bind off.

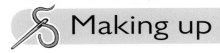

Making up

Sew in all the loose ends of yarn by threading them onto a large wool needle and taking them under several stitches to secure them, then trim off the excess yarn. To join up the cushions/pillows use mattress stitch, which gives an invisible seam.

Mattress stitch: Place the two seams to be joined side by side with the right sides of the fabric facing you. Thread a yarn needle with yarn. Insert the needle under the horizontal bar between the first stitch and the next stitch on one piece of fabric. Insert the needle under the same bar on the opposite piece of fabric. Continue working like this, pulling the yarn tight to bring the pieces together side by side as you work.

Join both the side seams like this leaving 10cm (4in) free to form the flap. Fold this over and catch into the side seams to form a pocket. For the Dark Blue cushion/pillow, sew buttons in position to correspond to the buttonholes on the flap. Insert the appropriate size of cushion pad/pillow form in each cover and fold over the flaps or do up the buttons. On the covers without buttonholes, sew on buttons as a decorative finish once you have secured the flaps.

Long ribbed scarf

This scarf is simple to knit, but it looks stylish and expensive – and it's wonderfully warm to wear.

Based on a version of double rib that is offset to form a textured rib and worked in double-knitting (light worsted) yarn, this simple scarf is soft and cosy.

The Yarn

Debbie Bliss Cashmerino DK is a luxurious blend of 55% merino wool with 33% microfibre and 12% cashmere. Its soft handle and large colour palette are ideal for cosy, colourful accessories.

GETTING STARTED

 A straight strip of ribbed fabric, this scarf is one of the easiest projects for beginners

Size:
Scarf is 20cm wide x 175cm long (8in x 69in)

How much yarn:
7 x 50g (2oz) balls of Debbie Bliss Cashmerino DK, approx 110m (120 yards) per ball

Needles:
Pair of 4mm (no. 8/US 6) knitting needles

Tension/gauge:
33 sts and 36 rows measure 10cm (4in) square over rib patt (stretched) worked on 4mm (no. 8/US 6) needles
IT IS ESSENTIAL TO WORK TO THE STATED TENSION/GAUGE TO ACHIEVE SUCCESS

What you have to do:
Cast on. Work in fancy rib pattern. Cast/bind off in rib pattern.

Abbreviations:
beg = beginning;
cm = centimetre(s);
cont = continue;
k = knit; **p** = purl;
patt = pattern;
rep = repeat;
RS = right side;
st(s) = stitch(es);
WS = wrong side

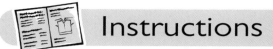

Instructions

SCARF:
Cast on 67 sts.
Work in rib patt as follows:
1st row: (RS) K3, *p2, k2, rep from * to end.
2nd row: K1, *p2, k2, rep from * to last 2 sts, p1, k1.
These 2 rows form rib patt. Cont in patt until Scarf
measures 175cm (69in) from beg, ending with a WS row.
Cast/bind off in rib patt.

 # Making up

Sew in loose ends of yarn.
Do not press.

HOW TO
WORK FANCY RIB

This simple rib stitch is made from a basic double rib, or knit 2, purl 2 rib, that is offset to form a textured pattern.

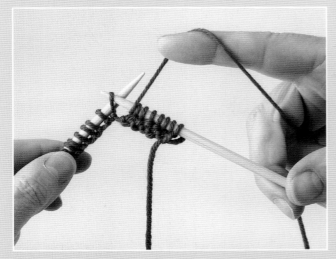

1 Begin row one by knitting three stitches. Purl two and knit two and then repeat this sequence to the end of the row.

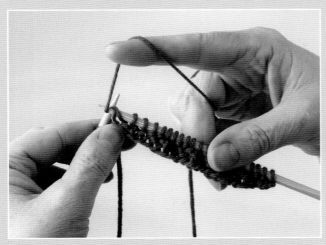

2 For the second row, begin with a knit stitch, then purl two and knit two to the last two stitches. Purl one and knit one to finish the row.

3 These two rows form the rib pattern and are repeated for the length of the scarf. As you work the rows you will be able to see the offset pattern emerging, which gives the rib a textured appearance.

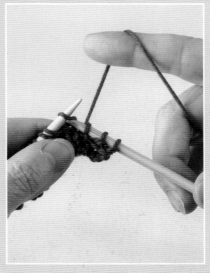

4 To make the edges of the scarf straight and neat you should tension/ gauge the yarn carefully at the beginning of each row. Starting from the first row, make sure that you gently pull the yarn as you make the first stitch to make a neat corner.

5 Keep the yarn well tensioned/ gauged between the first and second stitch on each row. This pulls the first stitch in tight, to give a neat edge without any loose loops.

Chunky shopping bag

An easy textured pattern and super-chunky yarn combine for a quick-to-make bag.

Quick and easy to knit, this neat shopping bag with a contrast-coloured top edge and button-trimmed handles is lined with fabric and practical to use.

GETTING STARTED

 Bag pattern is easy to follow with no shaping but simple sewing skills are necessary to finish off bag successfully

Size:

Bag is approximately 30cm wide x 28cm high x 7cm deep (12in x 11in x 2¾in)

How much yarn:

4 x 100g (3½oz) balls of Wendy Pampas Mega Chunky, approx 57m (62 yards) per ball in colour A

1 ball in colour B

Needles:

Pair of 8mm (no. 0/US 11) knitting needles

Additional items:

8 large buttons

50cm (20in) of cotton fabric 100cm (40in) wide, for lining

32cm x 8cm (12½in x 3in) rectangle of Bondaweb (fusible bonding web)

Matching sewing thread and needle

Cardboard

Tension/gauge:

13 sts and 27 rows measure 10cm (4in) square over patt on 8mm (no. 0/US 11) needles

IT IS ESSENTIAL TO WORK TO THE STATED TENSION/GAUGE TO ACHIEVE SUCCESS

What you have to do:

Work bag and handles in simple textured pattern. Make up bag as directed, sewing handles to outside of bag as shown. Sew fabric lining for bag and reinforce gusset with cardboard.

The Yarn

Wendy Pampas Mega Chunky contains 70% acrylic and 30% wool. It is a softly spun yarn with a distinctive twist that can be machine washed. There is a good range of natural shades and rustic contemporary colours.

Instructions

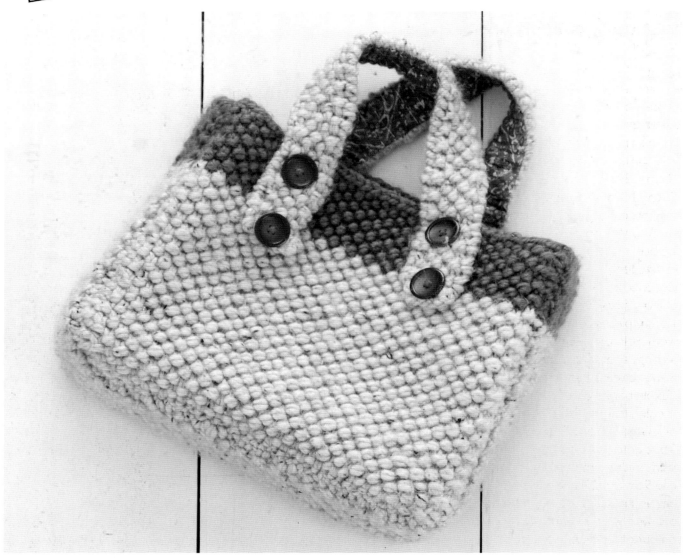

Abbreviations:

beg = beginning;
cm = centimetre(s);
cont = cotinue;
foll = follows; **k** = knit;
patt = pattern;
pwise = purlwise;
RS = right side;
sl = slip; **st(s)** = stitch(es);
WS = wrong side;
yfwd = yarn forward/ yarn over;
ytb = yarn to back

BACK:

With A, cast on 39 sts. Cont in patt as foll:
1st row: (RS) K1, (sl 1 pwise, k1) to end.
2nd row: K1, (yfwd, sl 1 pwise, ytb, k1) to end.
3rd row: K2, (sl 1 pwise, k1) to last st, k1.
4th row: K2, (yfwd, sl 1 pwise, ytb, k1) to last st, k1. These 4 rows form patt. Patt 52 more rows. Cut off A. Join in B and patt 20 more rows. Cast/bind off firmly.

FRONT:

Work as given for Back.

SIDES AND BASE GUSSET:

With B, cast on 9 sts. Work 20 rows in patt as given for Back. Change to A and patt another 56 rows. Insert a marker at each end of last row. Patt another 80 rows and insert a marker at each end of last row.
Patt 56 more rows.
Change to B and patt another 20 rows. Cast/bind off firmly.

HANDLES: (Make 2)

With A, cast on 7 sts. Cont in patt as given for Back until work measures

50cm (20in) from beg, ending with a WS row. Cast/bind off firmly.

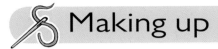

Making up

Using a flat stitch, join sides and base gusset to back and front, placing markers to bottom corners of back and front.

Lining:

From lining fabric, cut two 33cm x 31cm (13in x 12¼in) pieces for back and front and one 10cm x 89cm (4in x 35in) piece for gusset. Taking 1.5cm (⅝in) seam allowances, sew lining pieces together to form bag. Turn 1.5cm (⅝in) to WS around top edge of lining and sew in place.

Handles:

Cut two 6cm x 34cm (2½in x 13½in) pieces of lining fabric and two 4cm x 32cm (1½in x 12½in) pieces of Bondaweb (fusible bonding web). Fold under and press 1cm (⅜in) turnings all around lining pieces. Following manufacturer's instructions, iron Bondaweb (fusible bonding web) strips on to WS of handles, leaving 9cm (3½in) free at each end of knitted handles. Peel off paper and iron lining fabric onto this area. Neaten all around edge of fabric with a small hemming stitch. Positioning end 9cm (3½in) of handles on outside of bag as shown and leaving a 9cm (3½in) gap between them, sew handles onto bag. Sew on buttons, working through both thicknesses for strength.

Gusset:

Cut one 7cm x 30cm (2¾in x 12in) piece of cardboard for base and two 7cm x 28cm (2¾in x 11in) pieces for sides. Turn bag inside out, then with WS of lining and knitting together and working with RS of lining facing, catch stitch along two long seams of base, taking care not to go through to other side of knitted fabric. Slip base piece of cardboard in place between lining and knitting. Now catch stitch in same way along two seams of each side seam and slip two side pieces of cardboard in place. Hem lining in place all around top edge of bag, just below cast/bound-off row.

Greek-style rug

Knit this project with stretchy strips of fabric to make a stunning rag rug.

Try out a new technique with fabric scraps cut up into strips and knitted on jumbo needles to make this bright and stylish striped rug.

GETTING STARTED

Easiest garter stitch fabric but preparing fabric for knitting and working with large needles takes some getting used to

Size:
Rug is approximately 50cm wide x 76cm long (20in x 30in)

How much yarn:
2 x pairs of heart-print jersey pyjama trousers in sizes 14/16/US 12–14
2 x long-sleeved pink jersey tops in size 18/US 16
2 x short-sleeved purple jersey tops in size 16/US 14
1 x black and white striped short-sleeved jersey top in size 18/US 16
1 x black and white striped long-sleeved roll-neck jersey top in size 18/US 16
1m (1 yard) cotton jersey fabric 140cm (55in) wide in turquoise

Needles:
Pair of 12mm/US 17 knitting needles

Additional items:
Sharp dressmaking scissors
Ruler
Sewing needle and thread
Sewing machine

Tension/gauge:
10 sts and 16 rows measure 10cm (4in) square over g st on 12mm/US 17 needles
IT IS ESSENTIAL TO WORK TO THE STATED TENSION /GAUGE TO ACHIEVE SUCCESS

What you have to do:
Cut old clothing and fabric into strips for yarn
Work rug in garter stitch (every row knit) and stripes of fabric, knotting in each new colour at side edge.
Neaten by sewing in ends as instructed.

The Yarn
We used a combination of old and new clothing in jersey fabric and bought lengths of jersey fabric cut into strips. The old clothing can either come free from home, or you can buy from charity shops/thrift stores. If there is a particular colour that you want, then it is worth searching for it in low-price clothing stores.

Instructions

RUG:

First prepare all the garments and fabric being used, cutting them into strips. There are step-by-step instructions on preparing the yarn in the 'How to' panel on page 23.
With 12mm/US 17 needles and turquoise, cast on 50 sts. Work throughout in g st and stripe sequence as foll, knotting the yarns at the sides in the usual way when changing colour:

2 rows each turquoise, black and white stripes and pink
4 rows heart print
2 rows each purple and turquoise
4 rows black and white stripes
2 rows each pink, heart print and purple
Rep last 24 rows 4 times more.
Work 2 more rows in turquoise. Cast/bind off.

 # Making up

Undo any knots in yarns in body of rug and either machine or hand-sew end of fabric together close to surface of rug. Undo knots of colours changes down sides to a single tie and machine or hand-sew fabric ends together approximately 2cm (¾in) away from edge of rug. Fold sewn ends to WS and hand-sew to reverse of rug to neaten. Also sew ends from casting on and casting/binding off to WS of rug.

HOW TO
PREPARE THE FABRIC

Use nylon jersey to make this rug. You can buy the fabric by the metre/yard but you can also cut up old t-shirts and leotards and mix these fabrics with the shop-bought kind. Colours and patterns merge together when the rug is knitted but you can choose a palette of favourite shades.

1 Lay each piece of fabric out on a flat surface and with sharp scissors begin to cut into strips approximately 5cm (2in) wide.

3 Cut each piece of fabric in this way to make long strips of each colour or pattern. Wind the strips of fabric into individual balls.

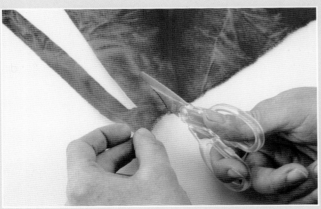

2 When you reach the end of the strip, stop cutting approximately 2cm (¾in) from the edge. Start cutting the next strip approximately 5cm (2in) along the edge. This gives a continuous strip of fabric.

4 Cast on and work the rug as instructed in garter stitch. Join each ball of fabric by knotting at the side of the work.

Signal flag bunting

Make a string of nautical-style bunting to decorate an outdoor party or to bring a seaside theme into a child's room.

This cheerful bunting in solid and patterned colours is easy to make in stocking/stockinette stitch with a crochet 'string' linking the pennants together. It will add a jolly touch to any outdoor occasion.

GETTING STARTED

 Simple stocking/stockinette stitch but some patterns are worked using the intarsia technique

Size:
Each pennant measures 11cm x 12cm (4¼in x 4¾in); completed strip with 12 pennants is approximately 186cm (73in) long

How much yarn:
1 x 50g (2oz) ball of Sirdar Luxury Soft Cotton DK, approx 95m (104 yards) per ball, in each of the following colours A, B, C, D and E

Needles:
Pair of 4mm (no. 8/US 6) knitting needles

Additional item:
4mm (no. 8/US 6) crochet hook

Tension/gauge:
22 sts and 28 rows measure 10cm (4in) square over st st using 4mm (no. 8/US 6) needles
IT IS ESSENTIAL TO WORK TO THE STATED TENSION/GAUGE TO ACHIEVE SUCCESS

What you have to do:
Work in stocking/stockinette stitch. Shape pennants with simple decreasing. Work colour patterns from charts, stranding yarn not in use across back of work. Crochet a chain to link pennants together.

The Yarn
Sirdar Luxury Soft Cotton is 100% pure cotton in a double knitting (light worsted) weight. Its bright colours are ideal for stocking/ stockinette stitch projects where the focal point is the colour work.

Instructions

Abbreviations:
cm = centimetre(s); **cont** = continue; **foll** = follows; **k** = knit; **p** = purl; **rem** = remain; **rep** = repeat; **RS** = right side; **skpo** = slip one stitch, knit one, pass slipped stitch over; **sk2po** = slip one stitch, knit 2 stitches together, pass slipped stitch over; **st(s)** = stitch(es); **st st** = stocking/stockinette stitch; **tbl** = through back of loops; **tog** = together; **WS** = wrong side

Note: When working from charts, read odd-numbered (RS) rows from right to left and even-numbered (WS) rows from left to right. Strand colours not in use loosely across WS of work.

BASIC PENNANT:
With yarn as given for each pennant below, cast on 25 sts. Work in st st, with shaping as foll:
1st row: (RS) K to end.
2nd row: K1, p to last st, k1.
3rd row: K1, skpo, k to last 3 sts, k2tog, k1.
4th row: As 2nd row.
5th row: As 1st row.
6th row: K1, p2tog, p to last 3 sts, p2tog tbl, k1.
Rep these 6 rows until 5 sts rem. Work 2 rows straight.
Next row: K1, sk2po, k1. 3 sts.
Work 1 row. K3tog and fasten off.

MAKE BUNTING:
Following instructions for Basic pennant, work each pennant as shown in the photograph on page 26. Top row left to right and then bottom row, left to right.

Red fleur-de-lys on white:
Work first 2 rows with B. Cont as Basic pennant, placing chart C on 3rd row as foll: k1, skpo, k2, work across

15 sts from 1st row of chart, k2, k2tog, k1. Cont as set, shaping pennant and working from chart until 25th row of chart has been completed.
Complete pennant with B.

Bermuda blue squares on red:
Work first 4 rows with A. Cont as Basic pennant, placing chart D on 5th row as foll: k4, work across 15 sts from 1st row of chart, k4. Cont as set, shaping pennant and working from chart until 16th row of chart has been completed.
Complete pennant with A.

Plain lemon:
Work with E only throughout.

Navy and bermuda blue stripes:
Cast on with D. Cont as Basic pennant, working in stripe patt of 4 rows D and 4 rows C until 7 stripes have been completed.
Complete pennant with C.

Lemon circle on red:
Work first 4 rows with A. Cont as Basic Pennant, placing chart E on 5th row as foll: k6, work across 11 sts from 1st row of chart, k6. Cont as set, shaping pennant and working from chart until 14th row of chart has been completed.
Complete pennant with A.

Quarters in white, navy and bermuda blue:
Cast on 13 sts with C and 12 sts with D. Cont as Basic pennant keeping continuity of colours as cast on until 15 rows have been completed. (15 sts)
16th row: P to end with C.
17th row: K7 C, 8 B.

Complete pennant with colours as set on 17th row.

Wide stripes:
Work first 12 rows with A, next 10 rows with B and complete pennant with C.

Plain bermuda blue:
Work with D only throughout.

White diamond on navy blue:
Work first 2 rows with C. Cont as Basic pennant, placing chart A on 3rd row as foll: k1, skpo, k2, work across 15 sts from 1st row of chart, k2, k2tog, k1. Cont as set, shaping pennant and working from chart until 15th row of chart has been completed.
Complete pennant with C.

Plain red:
Work with A only throughout.

Navy cross on lemon and bermuda blue:
Work first 2 rows with E. Cont as Basic pennant, placing chart B on 3rd row as foll: k1, skpo, k2, work across 15 sts from 1st row of chart, k2, k2tog, k1. Cont as set, shaping pennant and working from chart until 13th row of chart has been completed. With E, work 2 rows.
Change to D and complete pennant.

Plain navy:
Work with C only throughout.

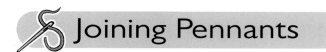

Joining Pennants

Darn in all loose ends on WS of pennants. Press carefully following instructions on ball band.
Arrange pennants in a row, as shown in photograph (above) or as required.

With 4mm (no. 8/US 6) crochet hook and B, make 30 chain, then working from right to left, work a row of double crochet (US single) across top of first pennant, make 6 chain, work in double crochet (US single) across top of second pennant, cont in this way until all pennants have been joined, work 30 chain. Fasten off.

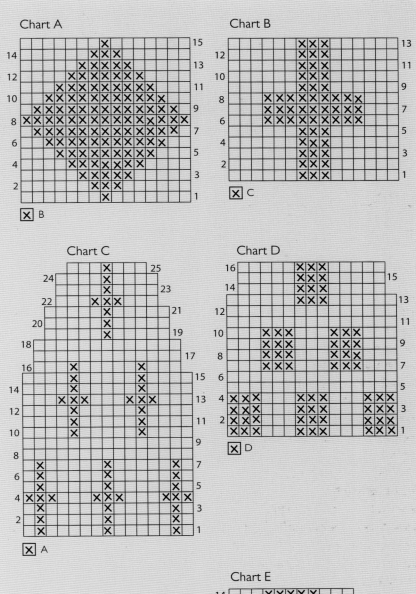

Chart A

Chart B

Chart C

Chart D

Chart E

HOW TO
WORK DOUBLE (US SINGLE) CROCHET

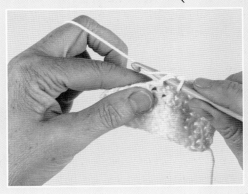

Insert the hook under both loops of the stitch below. Wrap the yarn around the hook and pull the yarn through the hole. There will be two loops on the hook. Wrap the yarn around the hook and pull this through both the loops to give a single loop on the hook. This completes one stitch.

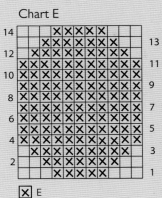

Diagonal-lace snood

Wrap this luxurious scarf twice around your neck for the ultimate cover-up.

A snood is a long, wide scarf joined into a circle that can be worn as a hood as well. This lacy one is knitted in a luxurious bouclé yarn to keep you extra warm and cosy.

GETTING STARTED

Straightforward but working with textured yarn and large needles needs patience

Size:
Snood is 38cm wide x 137cm all around (15in x 54in)

How much yarn:
4 x 50g (2oz) balls of Sublime Luxurious Woolly Merino, approx 90m (98 yards) per ball

Needles:
Pair of 6.5mm (no. 3/US 10½) knitting needles

Tension/gauge:
14 sts and 18 rows measure 10cm (4in) square over patt on 6.5mm (no. 3/US 10½) needles
IT IS ESSENTIAL TO WORK TO THE STATED TENSION/GAUGE TO ACHIEVE SUCCESS

What you have to do:
Cast on and Cast/bind off stitches very loosely. Work lace pattern with decorative increasing and decreasing as instructed. Sew short ends of strip together to form snood.

The Yarn
Sublime Luxurious Woolly Merino contains 96% merino wool and 4% nylon in a soft bouclé format. Machine washable, it is available in a palette of velvety wintery shades.

Abbreviations:

beg = beginning;
cm = centimetre(s);
k = knit; **p** = purl;
patt = pattern;
psso = pass slipped
stitch over;
rep = repeat;
RS = right side; **sl** = slip;
st(s) = stitch(es);
yfwd = yarn forward/yarn
over to make a stitch

Instructions

SNOOD:

Cast on 53 sts very loosely.

1st row: (RS) K2, (yfwd, sl 1, k1, psso, k1) to end.

2nd row: K2, p to last 2 sts, k2.

3rd row: K3, (yfwd, sl 1, k1, psso, k1) to last 2 sts, k2.

4th row: As 2nd row.

5th row: K4, (yfwd, sl 1, k1, psso, k1) to last st, k1.

6th row: As 2nd row.

These 6 rows form lace patt. Rep them until work measures 137cm (54in) from beg, ending with a RS row. Cast/bind off very loosely.

 # Making up

Do not press. Join two short ends using a flat seam.

HOW TO
USE BIG NEEDLES

Some beginners love using big needles and yarn because all the stitches are magnified and the knitting grows very quickly, while others find the size of the needles difficult to master. Here are some tips for using big needles and thick yarn.

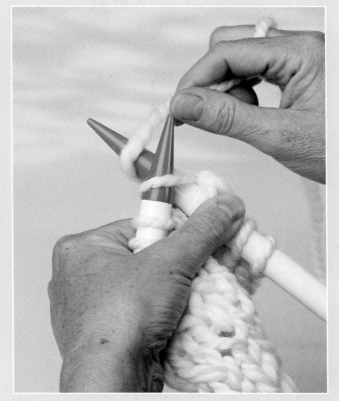

2 Hold both the needles in your left-hand while you wind the yarn around the needle to form the stitch. Large needles are not heavy so you can do this quite easily.

1 Try holding the right-hand needle with your hand over the needle rather than trying to hold it in a pen grip where the needle rests between your thumb and forefinger.

3 Make sure you keep the stitches on both needles near to the tip of the needles as you work. This means that your movements as you make the stitches and lift them from one needle to the other can be kept small. Stop and slide the stitches forward as needed.

Funky phone covers

Here's the ultimate project for the novice knitter – choose your favourite colour of yarn and get stitching!

These quirky covers will make a great talking point when you're out and about with friends. Worked in simple stitches and decorated with embroidery, they're very easy for beginners.

The Yarn

Sirdar Luxury Soft Cotton is 100% cotton in a double knitting (light worsted) weight. It has a soft, subtle sheen and is available in wide range of fashionable colours that are just right for these contemporary covers.

GETTING STARTED

 Both covers are really simple to make in basic stitches although the back of pink cover has vertical stripes where yarn is carried across wrong side of work

Size:
Red cover is 6.5cm x 12cm (2½in x 4¾in)
Pink cover is 6.5cm x 10cm (2½in x 4in)

How much yarn:
For the red cover:
1 x 50g (2oz) ball of Sirdar Luxury Soft Cotton DK, approx 95m (104 yards) per ball
Oddment of contrasting colour

For the pink cover:
1 x 50g (2oz) ball of Sirdar Luxury Soft Cotton DK in main colour A
Oddments of contrast colours B, C and D

Needles:
Pair of 4mm (no. 8/US 6) knitting needles

Additional items:
Button for each cover, blunt-ended needle with large eye for embroidery

Tension/gauge:
22 sts and 32 rows measure 10cm (4in) square over moss/seed st on 4mm (no. 8/US 6) needles
22 sts and 30 rows measure 10cm (4in) square over st st on 4mm (no. 8/US 6) needles
IT IS ESSENTIAL TO WORK TO THE STATED TENSION/ GAUGE TO ACHIEVE SUCCESS

What you have to do:
Work in moss/seed stitch. Make plaited/braided button loop. Overcast sides together. Work blanket stitch around flap. Work in stocking/stockinette stitch. Make narrow vertical stripes, stranding colour across wrong side of work. Work narrow horizontal stripes, carrying colours up side of work. Decorate with chain stitch embroidery. Make plaited/braided button loop.

 Instructions

Abbreviations:

beg = beginning; **cm** = centimetre(s); **cont** = continue;
foll = follows; **inc** = increase(ing); **k** = knit; **p** = purl;
patt = pattern; **rep** = repeat; **RS** = right side;
st(s) = stitch(es); **st st** = stocking/stockinette stitch;
WS = wrong side

RED COVER:

With red yarn, cast on 14 sts.

1st row: (RS) *K1, p1, rep from * to end.

2nd row: *P1, k1, rep from * to end.

Rep these 2 rows to form moss/seed st until work
measures 28cm (11in) from beg, ending with a WS row.
Cast/bind off in patt.

PINK COVER:
Front:

With A, cast on 10 sts.

1st row: (RS) K to end, inc in first and last sts.

2nd row: P to end.

3rd row: As 1st row. 14 sts.**

Beg with a p row, work 27 rows in st st, ending with a
WS row. Cast/bind off.

Back:

With A, cast on 10 sts. Join in B and cont as foll, stranding
yarn not in use loosely across WS of work:

1st row: (RS) With A, inc in first st, k1, with B, k2, k2 A,
2 B, with A, k1, inc in last st.

2nd row: P1 B, *2 A, 2 B, rep from * to last 3 sts, 2 A, 1 B.

3rd row: With B, inc in first st, *k2 A, 2 B, rep from * to
last 3 sts, k2 A, with B, inc in last st. 14 sts.

Beg with a p row and stripes as set, work 27 rows in st st,
ending with a WS row. Cast/bind off.

Gusset:

With A, cast on 6 sts. Beg with a k row and working in
stripe sequence of 2 rows each A, C, B and D, cont in st
st until gusset fits all around sides and shaped lower edge
of Front and Back, ending with a WS row and stripe in A.
Cast/bind off.

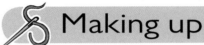 Making up

RED COVER:

Using the cast-on edge as top flap, fold two corners in
towards the centre so forming a V shape. Join the centre
seam created by overcasting.

Make button loop:

Knot 3 x 25cm (10in) lengths of contrasting colour yarn
together at one end. Insert free ends through a large-
eyed needle and thread down through pointed end of
flap so knot holds firmly in place. Plait/braid 3 strands
of yarn until they make a loop long enough to fit round
button, then thread ends back through flap and secure
with a knot.

Neatly sew down straight edge of flap on WS of cover.
Fold up cast/bound-off edge by 12cm (4¾in) and pin
side seams. With contrasting yarn, overcast side seams
together, working one stitch in from edges. With
contrasting yarn, blanket stitch around flap edges.
Fold down flap and mark position of button with a pin.
Sew on button.

PINK COVER:

Block and press according to directions on ball band.
Using photograph (right) as a guide, embroider three circles with D on Front.
Pin gusset in place around Front and sew in place with backstitch. Repeat with the Back.
Sew button to centre of top Front edge as shown.

Make button loop:

Knot 3 x 25cm (10in) lengths of A together at one end. Insert free ends through a large-eyed needle and thread through centre of top Back edge from WS so knot holds firmly in place. Plait/braid 3 strands of yarn until they make a loop long enough to fit around button, then thread ends back through same place and secure with a knot.

HOW TO
BACKSTITCH

Pin the pieces to be joined, right sides together, and try to match the edges, stitch for stitch.

1 To secure the yarn, bring the needle through from back to front and take the yarn around the outside edge. Bring the needle back through at the original point. Now take the yarn around the outside edge again and insert the needle from back to front one stitch width along to the left.

2 Insert the needle from front to back where the last stitch ended and then bring the needle to the front again one stitch further along. Tighten the yarn and repeat.

Checked dog coat

In trendy black and white, your adorable pooch will be the star attraction in his eye-catching winter coat.

Worked in stocking/stockinette stitch in an Op-art style black-and-white check, this is perfect for the dog about town.

GETTING STARTED

 Although the coat is a simple shape in stocking/stockinette stitch, following the chart and working the two-colour check pattern takes some skill

Size:
To fit toy[small:medium] sized dog
Coat width: 47[52:57]cm/18½[20½:22½]in
Length to tail: 28[38:43]cm/11[15:17]
Figures in square brackets [ ] refer to larger sizes; where there is only one set of figures, it applies to all sizes

How much yarn:
1 x 100g (3½oz) ball of Wendy Aran with Wool, approx 200m (219 yards) per ball, in each of colours A and B

Needles:
Pair of 4.5mm (no. 7/US 7) knitting needles
Pair of 5mm (no. 6/US 9) knitting needles
4.5mm (no. 7/US 7) circular knitting needle

Additional items:
Black elastic 2cm (¾in) wide
Black sewing thread
1 button, 1.5cm (⅝in) in diameter

Tension/gauge:
18 sts and 19 rows measure 10cm (4in) square over patt on 5mm (no. 6/US 9) needles
IT IS ESSENTIAL TO WORK TO THE STATED TENSION/GAUGE TO ACHIEVE SUCCESS

What you have to do:
Work in stocking/stockinette stitch and check pattern, working from chart. Strand colour not in use across back of work. Simple increasing and decreasing to shape coat. Pick up stitches around edges for ribbed neckband and borders.

The Yarn
Wendy Aran with Wool is a hard-wearing mixture of 75% acrylic with 25% wool – both practical and perfect for a dog coat that will need to be washed frequently. If you don't want a monochrome check pattern, then there are plenty of colours to choose from.

 ## Instructions

COAT:
Note: This is worked in one piece starting at tail.
With 5mm (no. 6/US 9) needles and A, cast on 40[46:52] sts. Cont in st st, beg with a k row, and check patt from chart, start at marked point as foll:
1st row: (RS) Work 20[23:26] sts of 1st row of chart reading from right to left, now work rem 20[23:26] sts reading same row of chart from left to right.
2nd row: Work 20[23:26] sts of 2nd row of chart reading from right to left, now work rem 20[23:26] sts reading same row of chart from left to right.
Cont in patt as set, rep 10 rows of chart and inc 1 st at each end of next and every row until there are 54[62:70] sts,

working extra sts into patt as shown on chart. Now inc 1 st at each end of every foll alt row until there are 78[86:96] sts, working extra sts into patt. Work straight until coat measures 26[36:41]cm/10¼[14¼:16¼]in from beg, ending with a WS row.

Shape shoulders and neck:

Next row: (RS) K2tog, patt 28[31:33] sts, turn and leave rem sts on a holder. Cont on these sts for first side.

Next row: Cast/bind off 2 sts, patt to end.

Next row: K2tog, patt to end.

Rep last 2 rows 4 times more. 14[17:19] sts. Now dec 1 st at each end of every RS row only until 8[11:11] sts rem. Cast/bind off.

Return to sts on holder. Slip first 18[20:26] sts on to a holder, rejoin yarn to next st, patt to last 2 sts, k2tog. Complete to match first side of neck, reversing shaping.

NECKBAND:

With 4.5mm (no. 7/US 7) needles, A and RS of work facing, pick up and k 20[24:28] sts down first side of neck, k across 18[20:26] sts from holder and pick up and k 20[24:28] sts up second side of neck. 58[68:82] sts.

Next row: *P1, k1, rep from * to end.

Rep last row 5 times more. Cast/bind off in rib.

OUTER BORDER:

With 4.5mm (no. 7/US 7) circular needle, A and RS of work facing, pick up and k 18[20:24] sts along first shoulder slope, 20[26:32] sts along straight side edge, 37[41:45] sts along

back slope, 38[44:50] sts across cast-on edge, 37[41:45] sts up lower slope, 20[26:32] sts along straight side edge and 18[20:24] sts along second shoulder slope. 188[218:252] sts. Work 4 rows in k1, p1 rib as given for Neckband. Cast/bind off in rib.

 # Making up

Join seam on collar, centre front and outer border to form a circle. Cut elastic to required length and stitch one end securely in place mid-way through straight side section (or at required position). Turn a small hem on other end of elastic and using yarn A, make a button loop on end of elastic. Sew button to inside of outer border to correspond.

A (black)   B (white)

10
9
8
7
6
5
4
3
2
1

Turn here

1st size 2nd size 3rd size   1st size 2nd size 3rd size

Beg and end here
on 1st & 2nd rows

Colourful cube

Get knitting with large needles and chunky yarn and then you'll literally be able to put your feet up!

Cover a foam cube with just six squares of stocking/stockinette stitch in clashing colours to make extra seating or a foot rest that's fun and funky. It couldn't be quicker or easier to do in this extra-chunky yarn.

The Yarn

Rowan Big Wool is 100% pure wool that is very chunky with a loose twist. It looks attractive and is very hard-wearing, especially for projects that will suffer wear and tear. There is a comprehensive shade range and plenty of choice for stripe sequences.

GETTING STARTED

 Very easy to make in stocking/stockinette stitch and chunky yarn but care must be taken for neat finish when joining seams

Size:

Cube is 30cm x 30cm x 30cm (12in x 12in x 12in)

How much yarn:

2 x 100g (3½oz) balls of Rowan Big Wool, approx 80m (87 yards) per ball

1 ball in each of colours A, B, D, E, F and G

Needles:

Pair of 10mm (no. 000/US 15) knitting needles

Additional items:

Large crochet hook

Foam cube measuring 30cm x 30cm x 30cm (12in x 12in x 12in)

Tension/gauge:

9 sts and 11 rows measure 10cm (4in) square over st st on 10mm (no. 000/US 15) needles

IT IS ESSENTIAL TO WORK TO THE STATED TENSION /GAUGE TO ACHIEVE SUCCESS

What you have to do:

Work in stocking/stockinette stitch. Follow stripe sequence, joining in and cutting off colours as required. Finish seams on right side of work by crocheting panels together.

Instructions

Abbreviations:
beg = beginning; **ch** = chain; **cont** = continue;
cm = centimetre(s); **dc** = double crochet/US; **sc** = single
crochet; **k** = knit; **ss** = slip stitch; **st(s)** = stitch(es);
st st = stocking/stockinette stitch

CUBE SIDE 1: (Make 2)
With A, cast on 28 sts. Beg with a k row, cont in st st
throughout and stripe sequence of: 6 rows A, 4 rows B, 10
rows C, 2 rows D, 6 rows E and 6 rows D. (34 rows in total).
Cast/bind off.

CUBE SIDE 2: (Make 2)
With F, cast on 28 sts. Beg with a k row, cont in st st throughout
and stripe sequence of: 10 rows F, 6 rows C, 1 row each D,
A, B, D, A, B and D, 7 rows A and 4 rows B. (34 rows in total).
Cast/bind off.

CUBE SIDE 3: (Make 2)
With E, cast on 28 sts. Beg with a k row, cont in st st throughout
and stripe sequence of: 4 rows E, 10 rows A, 2 rows C, 4 rows B, 4
rows C, 8 rows D and 2 rows C. (34 rows in total). Cast/bind off.

Making up

Sew in all yarn ends on wrong side of squares.
Place same squares on opposite sides of cube, with the
stitches running in opposite direction. Repeat to cover all
sides of cube and pin in place.
To join the seams, work all top square seams in one
piece and then all bottom square seams in one piece.
Finally join the side seams separately.
With crochet hook and G, work in dc (US sc) through
corresponding adjacent edges, 1 st in from the edge. At
corners, make 1 ch, work 1 dc (US sc) back into st just
worked, then continue along the next seam. Continue
around the square in this way, ending with 1 ch, ss in first
dc (US sc) worked. Fasten off.

HOW TO
CROCHET THE SEAMS TOGETHER

Join the seams of the squares as described in the making up instructions. Use a large crochet hook to decorate the seams with a row of double crochet (US single = sc).

1 Starting at the beginning of one seam, take the hook through both pieces of fabric just below the seam. Catch the yarn at the back of the fabric with the hook and pull the loop through to the right side. Take the hook back through both pieces of fabric, one stitch along to the left.

2 Catch the yarn with the hook and pull it through to the right side of the fabric. You will have two loops on the hook. Catch the yarn with the hook and draw it through the two loops. There will now be one loop on the crochet hook – one double crochet (US sc) is now complete.

3 Continue along the seam making a double crochet (US sc) stitch in each knitted stitch.

4 At the corner, make 1 chain stitch and then work a double crochet (US sc) stitch back into the stitch just worked.

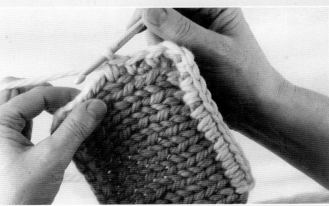

5 Continue along the next seam, forming a double crochet (US sc) stitch in the loops of the side of each stitch. Work around all the seams in this way.

Finger-free gloves

Stylish and comfortable, these cable-pattern gloves will keep you warm but leave your fingers free.

Be ultra trendy in these fabulous tweed gloves featuring an intricate cable panel on the back of the hand and cut-off fingers.

GETTING STARTED

Requires a lot of concentration with a fairly complicated cable panel and lots of shaping

Size:
One size to fit a woman's hand

How much yarn:
2 x 50g (2oz) balls of Debbie Bliss Donegal Luxury Tweed, approx 88m (96 yards) per ball

Needles:
Pair of 4.5mm (no. 7/US 7) knitting needles
Cable needle

Additional items:
2 large safety pins

Tension/gauge:
26 sts and 26 rows measure 10cm (4in) square over k2, p2 rib on 4.5mm (no. 7/US 7) needles
IT IS ESSENTIAL TO WORK TO THE STATED TENSION/GAUGE TO ACHIEVE SUCCESS

What you have to do:
Work palms in double (k2, p2) rib, while incorporating cable panel for back of hand. Shape for thumb gusset by making stitches and working gusset in reverse stocking/stockinette stitch. Shape fingers individually by picking up stitches and using turning rows over centre of work.

The Yarn
Debbie Bliss Donegal Aran Luxury Tweed contains 85% wool and 15% angora. It has the natural good looks and the distinctive flecked appearance of a tweed yarn. It comes in several fabulous shades.

Instructions

Abbreviations:

cn = cable needle; **cont** = continue; **foll** = follow(s)(ing); **inc** = increase(ing); **k** = knit; **m1** = make one stitch by picking up bar lying between needles and working into back of it; **p** = purl; **patt** = pattern; **rem** = remaining; **RS** = right side; **reverse st st** = reverse stocking/stockinette stitch (p side is RS); **sl** = slip; **st(s)** = stitch(es); **WS** = wrong side

C3B = sl next st on to cn and hold at back, k2, then p1 from cn

C3F = sl next 2 sts on to cn and hold at front, p1, then k2 from cn

C4B = sl next 2 sts on to cn and hold at back, k2, then k2 from cn

C4F = sl next 2 sts on to cn and hold at front, k2, then k2 from cn

C4BP = sl next 2 sts on to cn and hold at back, k2, then p2 from cn

C4FP = sl next 2 sts on to cn and hold at front, p2, then k2 from cn

CABLE PANEL: (Worked over 16 sts)

1st row: P6, k4, p6.
2nd and every foll WS row: K the k sts and p the p sts.
3rd row: P6, C4B, p6.
5th row: As 1st row.
7th row: As 3rd row.
9th row: P4, C4B, C4F, p4.
11th row: P3, C3B, k4, C3F, p3.
13th row: P2, C3B, p1, C4B, p1, C3F, p2.
15th row: P1, C3B, p2, k4, p2, C3F, p1.
17th row: P1, C3F, p2, C4B, p2, C3B, p1.
19th row: P2, C3F, p1, k4, p1, C3B, p2.
21st row: P3, C3F, C4B, C3B, p3.
23rd row: P4, C4FP, C4BP, p4.
25th–42nd rows: As 7th–24th rows.
43rd row: As 3rd row.
44th row: As 2nd row.

RIGHT GLOVE:

With 4.5mm (no. 7/US 7) needles cast on 44 sts. Place cable panel as foll:

1st row: (RS) P2, k2, work across next 16 sts as 1st row of cable panel, (k2, p2) 6 times.
2nd row: (K2, p2) 6 times, work across next 16 sts

as 2nd row of cable panel, p2, k2.
Cont in patt as now set until 20 rows have been worked.

Shape thumb:

Next row: P2, k2, work 16 sts of cable panel, k2, m1, p2, m1, patt to end.
Next row: Patt to end, working extra sts for thumb in reverse st st.
Next row: P2, k2, work 16 sts of cable panel, k2, m1, p4, m1, patt to end.
Next row: Patt to end, working extra sts for thumb in reverse st st.
Work a further 10 rows in patt, inc for thumb as set on 3rd, 5th, 7th and 9th rows. (There are now 14 sts for thumb.)
Next row: Patt 36 sts, turn and cast on one st, k15 (including cast-on st), turn and cast on one st, p16 (including cast-on st), turn.
Cont in reverse st st, work 3 rows on these 16 sts only. K 2 rows. Cast/bind off. **Oversew thumb seam.
With RS facing, re-join yarn and pick up 2 sts from base of thumb and patt to end. Cont in patt as set until 44th row of cable panel is complete.

Working in reverse st st only, cont as foll:

Next 2 rows: P to last 4 sts and sl these sts on to a safety pin, turn and k to last 4 sts and sl these sts on to a safety pin.

Shape first finger:

Next row: (RS) P24, turn and cast on one st, k13 (including cast-on st), turn and cast on one st, p14 (including cast-on st).

Cont in reverse st st, work 3 rows on these 14 sts only. K 2 rows. Cast/bind off. Oversew finger seam.

Shape second finger:

With RS facing, re-join yarn, pick up 2 sts from base of first finger and p to end. K 1 row.

Next row: (RS) P20, turn and k14, turn.

Cont in reverse st st, work 4 rows on these 14 sts only. K 2 rows. Cast/bind off. Oversew finger seam.

Shape third finger:

With RS facing, re-join yarn, pick up 2 sts from base of second finger and p to end. K 1 row.

Next row: (RS) P14, turn and k14.

Cont in reverse st st, work 4 rows on these 14 sts only. K 2 rows. Cast/bind off. Oversew finger seam.

Shape fourth finger:

With RS facing, re-join yarn, pick up 3 sts from base of third finger and then p4 sts on safety pin, turn and k7, then k rem 4 sts on safety pin. 11 sts. Cont in reverse st st, work 4 rows on these 11 sts only. K 2 rows. Cast/bind off.

Join seam along side of hand and darn in all loose ends.

LEFT GLOVE:

With 4.5mm (no. 7/US 7) needles cast on 44 sts. Place cable panel as foll:

1st row: (RS) (P2, k2) 6 times, work across next 16 sts as 1st row of cable panel, k2, p2.

2nd row: K2, p2, work across next 16 sts as 2nd row of cable panel, (p2, k2) 6 times.

Cont in patt as now set until 20th row of cable panel is complete.

Shape thumb:

Next row: (P2, k2) 5 times, m1, p2, m1, patt to end.

Next row: Patt to end, working extra sts for thumb in reverse st st.

Next row: (P2, k2) 5 times, m1, p4, m1, patt to end.

Next row: Patt to end, working extra sts for thumb in reverse st st.

Work a further 10 rows patt, inc for thumb as set on 3rd, 5th, 7th, and 9th rows. (There are now 14 sts for thumb.)

Next row: Patt 34 sts, turn and cast on one st, k14

(including cast-on st), turn and cast on one st, p16 (including cast-on st), turn.

Cont in reverse st st, work 3 rows on these 16 sts only. K 2 rows. Cast/bind off.

Complete as given for Right Glove from ** to end.

Quick-knit scarves

Choose the colour, pattern and width of your scarf and in next to no time you'll have it knitted.

Rows of knit stitches (known as garter stitch) form the pattern for these scarves. All you have to do is cast on, knit to the required length and then cast/bind off – it couldn't be easier.

GETTING STARTED

Straightforward stitch and chunky yarn makes these designs very quick to knit

Size:
*Wide scarf is 19cm wide x 150cm long
(7½in x 59in)
Skinny scarf is 10cm wide x 270cm long (4in x 106in)*

How much yarn:
*For the wide scarf:
4 x 50g (2oz) balls of Gedifra Baldini Colori, approx 45m (49 yards) per ball
5 x 50g (2oz) balls of Gedifra Extra Soft Merino Grande, approx 60m (66 yards) per ball*
*For the skinny scarf:
2 x 100g (3½oz) balls of Rowan Big Wool, approx 80m (87 yards) per ball*

Needles:
Pair of 15mm/US 19 knitting needles

Tension/gauge:
*Wide scarf: 7 sts and 11 rows measure 10cm (4in) square in g st on 15mm/US 19 needles using two strands of plain yarn and one strand of fancy yarn together
Skinny scarf: 7 sts and 12 rows measure 10cm (4in) square in g st on 15mm/US 19 needles*

What you have to do:
Cast on. Work in garter stitch (knit every row). Cast/bind off.

The Yarn
Wide scarf: Using two yarns together creates the unusual colouring and texture. Gedifra Baldini Colori is a fashion boucle yarn with variegated shading, while Gedifra Extra Soft Merino Grande is a smooth chunky yarn in a solid colour.
Skinny scarf: Rowan Big Wool is a loosely spun extra-chunky pure wool yarn in a solid colour. It gives good stitch definition and is incredibly warm.

Instructions

Abbreviations:
cm = centimetre(s);
 g st = garter stitch (every row knit)

WIDE SCARF:
Cast on 13 stitches using two strands of the plain yarn
and one strand of the fancy yarn together. Knit every
row to form garter stitch (g st) until scarf measures
150cm (59in).
Cast/bind off knitwise.

SKINNY SCARF:
Cast on 7 stitches.
Knit every row to form garter stitch (g st) until scarf
measures 270cm (106in).
Cast/bind off knitwise.

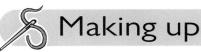 Making up

Sew in all the loose ends of yarn by threading them
onto a large wool needle and taking them under
several stitches to secure them, then trim off the
excess yarn. Follow the instructions on the ball band
for pressing the finished item, but it is not usually
necessary or advisable to press garter-stitch garments
like these scarves.

HOW TO
USE DIFFERENT YARNS TOGETHER

It is not uncommon to knit with several thicknesses of a yarn or to combine differnt types of yarn and to do this you just use two or more balls of yarn at a time. In this example, a textured yarn is worked with one ball of plain yarn. Our wide scarf uses two balls of plain yarn and one of textured yarn. Follow these tips for easy knitting.

▌ Take one end of each yarn you are using together, and unravel the amount you need to cast on from each ball.

2 Cast on in the usual way, the yarns will naturally twist together. Keep knitting with the strands of yarn together being careful that you do not miss one of the yarns when forming the stitches.

3 The balls will finish at different times as you knit the scarf. You can knot the ends together to join in a new ball and trim the ends up to the knot. The ends will add to the textured effect of the yarn.

Felted place settings

Co-ordinate the colours on your dining table with these quick-to-knit place mats and drinks coasters.

Add some fun to dining as well as padded practicality with this set of striped place settings. Easy to knit in a thick wool yarn, they are 'finished off' in the washing machine to achieve their felted appearance.

GETTING STARTED

The basic fabric for this could not be easier than garter stitch with no shaping involved but pay attention to felting as it is such a variable process

Size:
Placemats measure 28cm x 35cm (11in x 13¾in), after felting
Coasters are 9cm (3½in) in diameter, after felting

How much yarn:
For 4 place settings (4 mats and 4 coasters):
7 x 50g (2oz) balls of Twilleys Freedom Wool, approx 50m (55 yards) per ball, in each of colours A and B

Needles:
Pair of 8mm (no. 0/US 11) knitting needles

Tension/gauge:
13 sts and 22.5 rows measure 10cm (4in) square over g st on 8mm (no. 0/US 11) needles before felting
IT IS ESSENTIAL TO WORK TO THE STATED TENSION/GAUGE TO ACHIEVE SUCCESS

What you have to do:
Work in garter stitch (every row knit) throughout. Work in stripes of two colours. Felt finished fabrics in washing machine. Cut out circles from felted fabric for coasters. Decorate coaster edges with blanket stitch.

The Yarn
Twilleys Freedom Wool is 100% pure wool with a loosely spun construction that is ideal for felting as the fibres mesh together when it is washed in warm water. There is a good colour range to choose from, including several variegated shades as well.

Instructions

Abbreviations:

cm = centimetre(s); **cont** = continue; **foll** = follows;
g st = garter stitch (every row knit); **st(s)** = stitch(es)

PLACEMAT: (Make 4)

With A, cast on 42 sts. Cont throughout in g st, working
in stripe sequence of 2 rows each A and B, until 104 rows
have been worked. Cast/bind off.

COASTERS: (One piece of fabric makes 4 coasters)

With A, cast on 30 sts. Cont throughout in g st, working in
stripe sequence as foll: 10 rows A, 24 rows B, 10 rows A,
10 rows B, 24 rows A and 10 rows B. Cast/bind off.

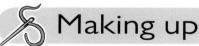

Making up

PLACEMAT:

To felt, machine-wash at 40°C (104°F). Reshape while
damp so that each piece measures approximately 30cm ×
36cm (12in × 14in) and dry flat. When dry trim edges to
28cm × 35cm (11in × 13¾in).

COASTERS:

To felt, machine-wash at 40°C (104°F). Reshape while
damp so that piece measures approximately 21cm × 30cm
(8in × 12in) and dry flat. Make a circular paper template
measuring 9cm (3½in) in diameter and, when dry, use
template to cut 4 circles from felted fabric. Cut circles so
that there is a wide stripe across centre of mat as shown in
photograph (above). Work blanket stitch around edges in
contrast colour.

HOW TO
BLANKET STITCH THE EDGES

Finish off the coasters by blanket stitching around the edge in one of the colours.

1 Felt the fabric for the coasters and then use a template to cut out the circles. Thread a blunt-ended needle with one of the two colours and knot the end. Bring the yarn through to the right side on the edge. Take the needle diagonally up to the right (this position will give the depth of the stitch and the width between stitches) and insert it into the fabric, bringing the needle out again through the edge.

2 Make sure the yarn is under the tip of the needle, so that it forms a loop, then pull the yarn through gently.

3 This forms the first stitch. Take the needle through the fabric diagonally to the right making sure that it is an equal distance to the first stitch. Pull the yarn gently to tighten the stitch.

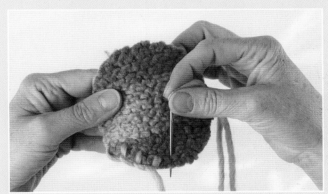

4 Continue in this way, working around the edge of the circle, keeping the stitches straight and evenly spaced. Tighten each stitch as you work to keep an even chain around the base of the stitches.

5 When you have completed the circle, knot the yarn at the back of the work, pushing the knot as tight as possible into the fabric. Trim both knots at the back and work them into the fabric so they are barely visible.

Exotic make-up bag

Hot colours, sewn-on sequins and fabric make a simple bag look glamorous and stylish.

Make this stunning zipped and lined make-up bag in easy stocking/ stockinette stitch and sizzling hot pink, purple and orange stripes, embellished with sew-on trimmings.

The Yarn
Debbie Bliss Prima is a luxurious mix of 80% bamboo and 20% merino wool. Its clear bright colours make this range perfect for colour work of any style.

GETTING STARTED

Straightforward striped stocking/stockinette stitch fabric with sewn-on embellishments

Size:
Make-up bag is 20.5cm wide x 14cm deep (8in x 5½in)

How much yarn:
1 x 50g (2oz) ball of Debbie Bliss Prima, approx 100m (109 yards) per ball, in each of three colours A, B and C

Needles:
Pair of 4mm (no. 8/US 6) knitting needles

Additional items:
1 pack of 8mm flat sequins in pink
1 pack of flat oval glass beads in orange
23cm (9in) embroidered ribbon, 30mm (1¼in) wide
20.5cm (8 in) zip fastener
30cm x 40cm (12in x 16in) rectangle of lining fabric
30cm x 40cm (12in x 16in) of lightweight, iron-on interfacing
Sewing needle and thread

Tension/gauge:
17 sts and 24 rows measure 10cm (4in) square over st st on 4mm (no. 8/US 6) needles
IT IS ESSENTIAL TO WORK TO THE STATED TENSION /GAUGE TO ACHIEVE SUCCESS

What you have to do:
Work in stocking/stockinette stitch and stripe pattern. Carry colours not in use up side of work. Sew on sequins, beads and ribbon to decorate. Sew a simple fabric lining. Insert a zip fastener into opening.

Abbreviations:
beg = beginning;
cm = centimetre(s);
cont = continue;
foll = follows;
k = .knit;
patt = pattern;
RS = right side;
st(s) = stitch(es);
st st = stocking/
stockinette stitch;
WS = wrong side

Instructions

BAG: (Worked in one piece)
With A, cast on 36 sts.
Beg with a k row, cont in st st and stripe patt as foll:
*4 rows A
1 row each B and C
2 rows B
4 rows C
3 rows A
1 row each B and C
2 rows A
5 rows C
1 row B
5 rows A**
8 rows C
Now work as given from ** back to *, so working stripes in reverse order. Cast/bind off with A.

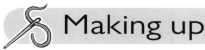

Making up

Press according to directions on ball band.
Lining: Following manufacturer's instructions, iron interfacing on to back of lining fabric. Using pressed bag as a

template, cut out lining fabric, adding 1.5cm (⅝in) extra all around for turnings. Turn 1.5cm (⅝in) to WS along the short edges of lining and press. With RS facing, fold lining in half and join side seams, taking 1.5cm (⅝in) seam allowances.

Bag: Using sewing thread in matching colour and referring to photograph as guide, sew two rows of beads and two rows of sequins along stripes, sewing one bead or sequin into each stitch (except for 1st and last stitch). Sew the ribbon on top of a stripes, taking care not to pucker the knitted fabric. With RS facing, fold bag in half and join side seams, enclosing raw ends of ribbon. Turn RS out and pin the zip along each of the top edges, not too close to the zip teeth. Sew into place. With WS of bag and lining facing, insert lining in bag. Matching side seams, pin top of lining around top of bag, covering edge of zip tape but not too close to teeth. Slip stitch lining in place.

HOW TO
CARRY COLOURS UP THE SIDE

When you are knitting a piece of fabric with narrow stripes of colour it is easier to carry the yarn of the individual colours up the side of the fabric instead of cutting and rejoining the yarn for each stripe.

1 Start a new colour by knotting the yarn around the yarn of the previous colour at the side of the fabric. Slide the knot right up under the last stitch knitted on the row.

2 Knit the row in the new colour and continue as instructed to make the stripe the correct width. Do not cut the yarn when you have completed the stripe.

3 Pick up the yarn from a previous stripe. Insert the right-hand needle into the first stitch and carry the yarn up the side of the work and wrap it around the needle to make the first stitch. Make sure you leave a loop of yarn that is the length of

the width of the stripe; if it is too tight the edge of the fabric will pucker and if it is too loose then you will end up with untidy large loops of yarn at the sides. Continue in this way, carrying the individual colours up the side of the fabric for each stripe.

Textured table runner

You can extend this runner by adding further panels of coloured and textured stitches.

Jazz up the dining table with this brightly-striped cotton runner that's a sampler of different basic fabrics and textured patterns.

GETTING STTARTED

This straight strip with colour blocks of basic stitches is perfect for a novice knitter, but care must be taken to keep the knitting neat

Size:
Runner is 25cm wide x 81cm long (10in x 32in)

How much yarn:
2 x 50g (2oz) balls of Debbie Bliss Cotton DK, approx 84m (92 yards) per ball, in colour A
1 ball in each of colours B, C, D and E

Needles:
Pair of 4mm (no. 8/US 6) knitting needles

Tension/gauge:
18 sts and 27 rows measure 10cm (4in) square over st st on 4mm (no. 8/US 6) needles
IT IS ESSENTIAL TO WORK TO THE STATED TENSION/GAUGE TO ACHIEVE SUCCESS

What you have to do:
Work in stripes of five colours and different stitch patterns. Join in and cut off colours as required. Work in moss/seed stitch. Work in garter stitch. Work in diagonal rib pattern. Work in woven pattern.

The Yarn
Debbie Bliss Cotton DK is a 100% cotton yarn with a slight twist to the fibres that is perfect for textured patterns. There is a fabulous colour range so you can choose all your favourite bright shades.

 # Instructions

Abbreviations:

cm = centimetre(s);

g st = garter stitch (every row knit); **k** = knit; **p** = purl;

patt = pattern; **rep** = repeat; **RS** = right side;

st(s) = stitch(es); **st st** = stocking/stockinette stitch;

WS = wrong side

RUNNER:

With A, cast on 46 sts using the thumb method.

Cut off A and join in B. K 1 row.

Next row: (WS) *K1, p1, rep from * to end.

Next row: *P1, k1, rep from * to end.

Rep last 2 rows to form moss/seed st until 23 rows in all have been worked, ending with a WS row.

Cut off B and join in A. Work 18 rows in g st, ending with a WS row.

Cut off A and join in C. K 1 row. Cont in diagonal rib patt.

1st row: (WS) K2, *p3, k3, rep from * to last 2 sts, p2.

2nd row: K3, *p3, k3, rep from * to last st, p1.

3rd row: *P3, k3, rep from * to last 4 sts, p3, k1.

4th row: P2, *k3, p3, rep from * to last 2 sts, k2.

5th row: P1, *k3, p3, rep from * to last 3 sts, k3.

6th row: K1, *p3, k3, rep from * to last 3 sts, p3.

Rep these 6 rows to form diagonal rib patt until 20 rows in all have been completed, ending with a RS row.

Cut off C and join in D. P 1 row.

Work 24 rows in moss/seed st, ending with a WS row.

Cut off D and join in E. Work 16 rows in g st, ending with a WS row.

Cut off E and join in A. K 1 row. Cont in woven patt.

1st row: (WS) *K5, p3, rep from * to last 6 sts, k6.

2nd row: P6, *k3, p5, rep from * to end.

3rd row: As 1st row.

4th row: K to end.

5th row: K1, *p3, k5, rep from * to last 5 sts, p3, k2.

6th row: P2, *k3, p5, rep from * to last 4 sts, k3, p1.

7th row: As 5th row.

8th row: K to end.

Rep these 8 rows to form woven patt until 31 rows in all have been completed, ending with a WS row.

Cut off A and join in E. Work 16 rows in g st, ending with a WS row.

Cut off E and join in D. K 1 row. Work 25 rows in moss/seed st, ending with a WS row.

Cut off D and join in C. K 1 row. Work 21 rows in diagonal rib patt, ending with a WS row.

Cut off C and join in A. Work 18 rows in g st, ending with a WS row.

Cut off A and join in B. K 1 row. Work 23 rows in moss/seed st, ending with a WS row.

Cut off B and join in A. K 1 row. Cast/bind off knitwise.

 ## Making up

Weave in all ends of yarn.
Pin out to finished size and, if necessary, press lightly with a warm iron over a dry cloth, taking care not to flatten the stitches.

Zipped shoulder bag

Make this bag in a bright colour to accessorize your favourite shirt or top.

For the latest in trendy accessories, just slip this bag over your shoulder and across your body. Worked in easy stocking/stockinette stitch, it has a zipped opening to keep your belongings safe.

GETTING STARTED

Bag consists of easy straight pieces of stocking/stockinette stitch, but care will be needed with the construction and making up

Size:

Bag is 20cm wide x 23cm high (8in x 9in)

How much yarn:

4 x 50g (2oz) balls of Debbie Bliss Cotton DK, approx 84m (92 yards) per ball, in turquoise

Needles:

Pair of 4mm (no. 8/US 6) knitting needles

Additional items:

20.5cm (8in) zip fastener

125cm (50in) of webbing, 4cm (1½in) wide to strengthen straps

24cm x 50cm (9½in x 20in) rectangle of lining fabric (optional)

20cm x 23cm (8in x 9in) rectangle of heavyweight interfacing or thick card for stiffening (optional)

Tension/gauge:

20 sts and 28 rows measure 10cm (4in) square over st st on 4mm (no. 8/US 6) needles

IT IS ESSENTIAL TO WORK TO THE STATED TENSION/ GAUGE TO ACHIEVE SUCCESS

What you have to do:

Work straight pieces in stocking/stockinette stitch. Sew in zip fastener. Make fabric lining (optional).

The Yarn

Debbie Bliss Cotton DK is 100% cotton with a slight twist to the fibres. Its excellent quality is perfect for good-looking stocking/ stockinette stitch fabrics and the comprehensive colour range is great for matching up knitted accessories to existing outfits.

Abbreviations:

beg = beginning;
cm = centimetre(s);
k = knit;
p = purl;
RS = right side;
st(s) = stitch(es);
st st = stocking/
stockinette stitch;
WS = wrong side

Instructions

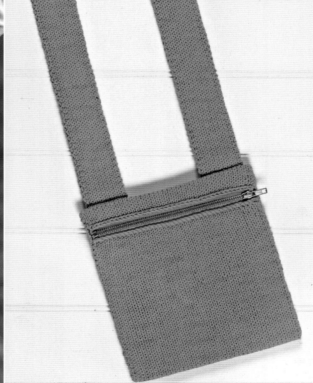

BAG:

Cast on 40 sts. Beg with a k row, work 45cm (18in) in st st, ending with a p row. Cast/bind off neatly.

STRAPS: (Make 2)

Cast on 10 sts. Beg with a k row, work 122cm (48in) in st st, ending with a p row. Try strap over one shoulder and across body to check it is the correct length and then shorten or lengthen as required. Cast/bind off.

Making up

Press pieces according to directions on ball band. Place one strap on top of the other with WS facing and join together along both long edges using a neat running stitch. Thread webbing through strap and trim the ends level. Turn ends of zip tape to WS to neaten and secure with a few stitches. Place the zip to WS of bag piece so joining cast-on and cast-off edges. Pin in place so cast-on edge is about 5mm (¼in) away from zip teeth. Sew zip in place. Repeat for other side of zip.

Lining: (Optional)

Measure width and length (from cast-on to cast/bound-off edge) of bag and cut a piece of lining fabric, adding 1cm (⅜in) seam allowance on to all edges. Turn under seam allowance along short edges. Pin one of these edges, with WS facing, on to the zip, keeping same distance from teeth as knitted piece, and sew in place. Repeat for the other side. With RS together, fold lining so zip is 2.5cm (1in) below top edge and the base is about 23cm (9in) below top edge. Join side seams of lining.

Make up knitted pieces as foll:

With WS together, fold bag so zip is 2.5cm (1 in) below top edge and base is about 23cm (9in) below top edge. Working from RS, join one side of bag with a neat running stitch. Push piece of stiffening into back of bag (behind lining, if used). Join the other side seam. Place bag RS down on a flat surface and measure 2.5cm (1in) down from top edge of back and place markers. Sew one end of strap securely to the bag, placing the edge to marker and side of strap to side of bag. Repeat for other end of strap, taking care not to twist strap.

Four seasons egg cosies

Brighten up breakfast with these egg cosies. Use them together or save your individual cosy for the correct season!

Breakfast eggs will be a real treat with this set of colourful mini hats that reflect the seasons.

GETTING STARTED

Each cosy is simple to make, but take care with the details for a professional finish

Size:
Each cosy measures 13cm (5in) in circumference by about 8cm (3in) in depth, minus trimmings

How much yarn:
1 x 50g (2oz) ball of Patons Diploma Gold DK, approx 120m (131 yards) per ball, in each of the following colours
Spring: *A, B and C; small amount of contrasting shade for chick's feet and beak*
Summer: *D, E and F*
Autumn/Fall: *G, H, I and J*
Winter: *K*

Needles:
Pair of 4mm (no. 8/US 6) knitting needles
Pair of 4mm (no. 8/US 6) double-ended knitting needles (Spring), Cable needle (Winter)

Tension/gauge:
25 sts and 34 rows measure 10cm (4in) square over st st on 4mm (no. 8/US 6) needles
IT IS ESSENTIAL TO WORK TO THE STATED TENSION/ GAUGE TO ACHIEVE SUCCESS

What you have to do:
Work Spring Cosy in single rib and stocking/stockinette stitch with intarsia spots; knit chick for top. Work Summer Cosy in stocking/stockinette stitch; knit flower for top and embroider flower border and blanket stitch edging. Work Autumn/Fall Cosy in double rib and stocking/stockinette stitch stripes; make tassel for top. Work Winter Cosy in garter stitch and cable pattern; make pompom for top and garter-stitch 'scarf'.

The Yarn
Patons Diploma Gold DK is a practical mixture of 55% wool, 25% acrylic and 20% nylon. It is ideal for items that will need cleaning as it can be machine washed. There is a good palette with plenty of choice for this colourful set.

Instructions

Abbreviations:
alt = alternate; **beg** = beginning; **cm** = centimetre(s); **cont** = continue; **C2F** = slip next st on cable needle and leave at front, k1, then k1 from cable needle; **foll** = follow(s)(ing); **g st** = garter stitch; **inc** = increase(ing); **k** = knit; **p** = purl; **patt** = pattern; **psso** = pass slipped stitch over; **rem** = remaining; **rep** = repeat; **RS** = right side; **sl** = slip; **st(s)** = stitch(es); **st st** = stocking/stockinette stitch; **tog** = together; **WS** = wrong side

5th row: (Sl 1, k1, psso, k2tog) 4 times.
7th row: (K2tog) to end. 4 sts.
8th row: (P2tog) to end. 2 sts.
Pass 2nd st over 1st and fasten off.

SUMMER COSY:

With 4mm (no. 8/US 6) needles and E, cast on 32 sts. Beg with a k row, work 2 rows in st st. Cut off E. Cont in D, work 16 rows in st st.

Shape top:

Work as given for Spring cosy.

AUTUMN/FALL COSY:

With 4mm (no. 8/US 6) needles and H, cast on 32 sts. Join in G.

1st row: (RS) With G, (k2, p2) to end.
2nd row: As 1st row.
3rd row: With I, as 1st row.
4th row: With G, as 1st row.
5th row: As 1st row.
6th row: With J, as 1st row.
Beg with a k row, cont in st st and work 10 rows in stripes as foll: 2 rows G; 1 row H; 2 rows G; 1 row I; 2 rows G; 1 row J; 1 row G.

Shape top:

Beg with 1 row G, cont in stripes as set, work as given for Spring cosy.

SPRING COSY:

With 4mm (no. 8/US 6) needles and A, cast on 32 sts. Work 4 rows in k1, p1 rib. K 1 row and p 1 row. Join in B. Cont in st st and stranding yarn not in use across back of work, work 8 rows in spot patt from chart, then rep 1st and 2nd rows again. Work 2 more rows from chart, shaping as foll, then cut off B and cont in A.

Shape top:

1st row: (Sl 1, k1, psso, k4, k2tog) 4 times.
2nd and foll alt rows: P to end.
3rd row: (Sl 1, k1, psso, k2, k2tog) 4 times.

WINTER COSY:

With 4mm (no. 8/US 6) needles and K, cast on 32 sts. K 5 rows. Cont in cable patt:

1st row: (WS) P2, (k1, p2, k1, p4) to last 6 sts, (k1, p2) twice.
2nd row: K2, (p1, k2, p1, k4) to last 6 sts, (p1, k2) twice.
3rd row: As 1st row.
4th row: K2, (p1, C2F, p1, k4) to last 6 sts, p1, C2F, p1, k2.
5th row: As 1st row.
6th row: As 4th row.
7th–8th rows: As 1st and 2nd rows.
9th row: As 1st row.
10th row: As 4th row.
11th row: As 1st row.
12th row: (Sl 1, k1, psso, p1, C2F, p1, k2tog) 4 times. 24 sts.

Shape top:

Beg with 2nd row, work as given for Spring cosy.

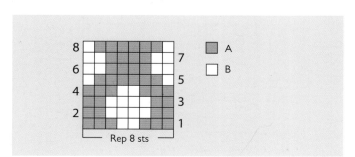

 Making up

SPRING COSY:
Join back seam.
Chick:
With 4mm (no. 8/US 6) double-pointed needles and C, cast on 8 sts. K 6 rows to form tube, sliding sts along needle and pulling yarn around to other side at end of each row. Cast/bind off. Gather both ends and wrap some yarn around tube to form the chick's neck. Sew chick to top of cosy, adding 3 straight sts for each foot and a small loop for beak.

SUMMER COSY:
Join back seam.
Flower:
With 4mm (no. 8/US 6) needles and E, cast on 3 sts.
1st–3rd rows: Inc in 1st st, k to end. 6sts. Cut off yarn and leave sts on needle.
Make 4 more 'scallops', casting on to empty needle.
4th row: K across all 5 scallops. 30 sts.
5th row: (K2tog) to end. 15 sts.
6th row: (K2tog) to last st, k1. 8 sts.
7th row: As 5th row. 4 sts.
Cut off yarn. Thread cut end through rem sts and draw up. Join flower seam and attach to top of cosy. Decorate flower centre with a French knot worked in D.

Embroidery:
With E used double, work blanket stitch along cast-on edge. Work 8 flowers as shown in photograph (above) – using E, work 5 petals in lazy daisy stitch, with a French knot centre in D and a detached chain-stitch leaf in F.

AUTUMN/FALL COSY:
Join back seam.
Tassel:
Cut six 12cm (5in) lengths of G and three each of H, I and J. Fold in half and tie at top, then wrap yarn G 1cm (½in) ldown from top to form tassel. Trim to about 5cm (2in) long. Attach to top of cosy.

WINTER COSY:
Join back seam. Make a pompom in K and attach to top of cosy.
Scarf:
With 4mm (no. 8/US 6) needles and K, cast on 4 sts. Work 40 rows in g st. Cast/bind off. Fold in half and sew fold to centre front of cosy over lower band.

Beanie hat

A classic beanie hat is a must for every wardrobe and it makes the perfect gift.

Pull on this ribbed beanie with its turn-back brim. Knitted in a soft Aran yarn, it will keep you warm and cosy.

GETTING STARTED

This hat is so quick and easy that it is perfect for a beginner

Size:
To fit an average size head

How much yarn:
2 x 50g (2oz) balls of Debbie Bliss Cashmerino Aran, approx 110m (120 yards) per ball

Needles:
Pair of 4.5mm (no. 7/US 7) knitting needles
Pair of 5mm (no. 6/US 8) knitting needles

Tension/gauge:
19 sts and 25 rows measure 10cm (4in) square over patt on 5mm (no. 6/US 8) needles
IT IS ESSENTIAL TO WORK TO THE STATED TENSION/GAUGE TO ACHIEVE SUCCESS

What you have to do:
Work in k1, p3 rib. Keep knit ribs correct throughout, shape crown within purl panels.

The Yarn
Debbie Bliss Cashmerino Aran is a luxurious mixture of 55% merino wool, 33% microfibre and 12% cashmere. It can be machine washed at a cool temperature and there is a large range of fabulous colours to choose from.

Abbreviations:
beg = beginning;
cm = centimetre(s);
k = knit;
p = purl;
patt = pattern;
psso = pass slipped
stitch over;
rem = remaining;
rep = repeat;
RS = right side;
st(s) = stitch(es);
sl = slip;
tog = together;
WS = wrong side

Instructions

HAT:
With 4.5mm (no. 7/US 7) needles cast on 101 sts.
1st row: (RS) P2, (k1, p3) to last 3 sts, k1, p2.
2nd row: K2, (p1, k3) to last 3 sts, p1, k2.
Rep these 2 rows to form rib patt. Work 2 more rows.
Change to 5mm (no. 6/US 8) needles. Work 19 more rows
in patt, ending with a RS row. Beg with 1st row again to
reverse fabric for brim, patt 22 rows, ending with a
WS row.

Shape crown:
1st row: P2, (k1, p2tog, p1, k1, p3) to last 3 sts, k1, p2tog.
88 sts.
2nd row: K1, (p1, k3, p1, k2) to last 3 sts, p1, k2.
Rib 2 more rows as set.
5th row: P2tog, (k1, p2, k1, p2tog, p1) to last 2 sts, k1, p1.
75 sts.
6th row: K1, (p1, k2) to last 2 sts, p1, k1.
Rib 2 more rows as set.
9th row: P1, (k1, p2tog, k1, p2) to last 2 sts, k1, p1. 63 sts.
10th row: K1, (p1, k2, p1, k1) to last 2 sts, p1, k1.
Rib 2 more rows as set.

BEGINNERS' STITCH GUIDE

KNIT ONE, PURL THREE RIB

This hat is worked in knit one, purl three rib, which makes it stretchy as well as giving the fabric a distinctive pattern. The rib pattern is worked over an odd number of stitches and two rows. Begin the first row with purl two and then repeat a sequence of knit one, purl three to the last three stitches; end with knit one and purl two. On the second row begin with knit two and then work a purl one, knit three rib to the last three stitches; end with purl one and knit two.

13th row: P1, (k1, p1, k1, p2tog) to last 2 sts, k1, p1. 51 sts.
14th row: K1, (p1, k1) to end.
15th row: P1, (sl 1, k2tog, psso, p1) to last 2 sts, k2tog. 26 sts.
16th row: (P1, k1) to end.
17th row: (P1, sl 1, k2tog, psso) to last 2 sts, k2tog. 13 sts.
18th row: K1, (p1, k1) to end.
Cut off yarn, thread through rem sts, draw up and fasten off securely.

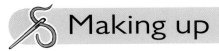 Making up

Do not press. Join back seam, reversing seam for last 9cm (3½in) for brim.

Cable-trimmed slippers

Knit these fun slippers in different colours for every member of the family!

Knitted in two clashing colours with a raised central cable, these comfortable slippers are eye-catching as well as warm and cosy.

GETTING STARTED

Knitted sections are fairly easy but making up slippers requires neat assembly

Size:
To fit shoe sizes: 37[38:39]/UK 4[5:6]/US 6½[7½:8½]
Length: approximately 22[24:26]cm/8½[9½:10¼]in
Note: Figures in square brackets [ ] refer to larger sizes; where there is only one set of figures only, it applies to all sizes

How much yarn:
2 x 50g (2oz) balls of Debbie Bliss Cashmerino DK, approx 110m (120 yards) per ball, in each of two colours A and B

Needles:
Pair of 3.75mm (no. 9/US 5) knitting needles
Cable needle

Additional items:
Sheet of 2mm (⅛in) thick craft and hobby foam for soles

Tension/gauge:
24 sts and 30 rows measure 10cm (4in) square over st st on 3.75mm (no. 9/US 5) needles
IT IS ESSENTIAL TO WORK TO THE STATED TENSION/GAUGE TO ACHIEVE SUCCESS

What you have to do:
Work front of slippers in ridge patt with central cable and shaping as instructed. Work front linings and upper soles in stocking/stockinette stitch. Work lower soles in reverse stocking/stockinette stitch. Use soles as templates to cut foam linings. Sew together slippers as instructed. Make twisted cords with pompon trims to decorate cables.

The Yarn
Debbie Bliss Cashmerino DK is a luxurious mixture of 55% merino wool, 33% microfibre and 12% cashmere. It can be washed at a low temperature and there is a wide choice of shades to create interesting colour combinations.

Instructions

Abbreviations:

alt = alternate; **beg** = beginning;
CF4 = sl next 2 sts on to cable needle and hold at front, k2, then k2 from cable needle
cm = centimetre(s); **cont** = continue;
dec = decrease; **foll** = follow(s)(ing);
inc = increase; **k** = knit; **m l** = make one stitch by picking up strand lying between needles and working into back of it; **p** = purl;
patt = pattern; **rem** = remain; **rep** = repeat;
sl = slip; **st(s)** = stitch(es); **st st** = stocking/ stockinette stitch; **tbl** = through back of loops;
tog = together; **WS** = wrong side

FRONT: (Make 2)

With 3.75mm (no. 9/US 5) needles and A, cast on 35[39:43] sts.
1st row: (RS) P1, *k1, p1, rep from * to end.
2nd row: K1, *p1, k1, rep from * to end.
Rep these 2 rows once more, then work 1st row again.
Inc row: (WS) Rib 16[18:20], (m1, rib 1) 3 times, rib to end. 38[42:46] sts. Now cont in patt as foll:
1st row: (RS) K to end.
2nd row: P to end.
3rd row: P17[19:21], C4F, p17[19:21].
4th row: K17[19:21], p4, k17[19:21].
Rep these 4 rows 7 times more.
Shape front:
Next row: (RS) K2tog, k13[15:17], k2tog tbl, k4, k2tog, k13[15:17], k2tog.
Next row: P to end.
Next row: P2tog, p11[13:15], p2tog, C4F, p2tog, p11[13:15], p2tog.
Next row: K13[15:17], p4, k13[15:17].
Cont to dec 4 sts on every RS row as now set – 1 st at each end of row and 1 st at either side of centre 4-st cable – until 14[10:10] sts rem. Patt 1 row. Cast/bind off.

FRONT LINING: (Make 2)

With 3.75mm (no. 9/US 5) needles and B, cast on 35[39:43] sts. Work 6 rows in k1, p1 rib as given for Front, inc 1 st at each end of last row. 37[41:45] sts.
Beg with a k row, cont in st st until work measures 9cm (3½in) from beg, ending with a p row. Now dec 1 st at

each end of every row until 15[11:11] sts rem.
Cast/bind off.

UPPER SOLE: (Make 2)

With 3.75mm (no. 9/US 5) needles and B, cast on 10[12:12] sts and beg at toe end. Beg with a k row, cont in st st, inc 1 st at each end of 2nd and every foll alt row until there are 20[24:26] sts, then at each end of every foll 4th row until there are 24[28:30] sts.
Work straight until sole measures 19[21:22] cm/7½[8¼:8¾]in from beg, ending with a p row. (Note that sole can be lengthened or shortened here as required. Keep a note of number of rows worked here to ensure that all 4 sole pieces are exactly the same.)
Shape heel:
Dec 1 st at each end of next and every foll alt row until 16[20:22] sts rem, then at each end of every row until 10[12:12] sts rem. Cast/bind off.

LOWER SOLE: (Make 2)

Work as given for Upper sole, but using A and working in reverse st st.

Making up

Using knitted soles as a template, cut two pieces of craft and hobby foam to the correct size and shape. With RS together, use backstitch to sew front to toe end of lower sole. Turn RS out. Join front lining and upper sole in the same way. Do not turn through, but slip lining into front with ribbed edges matching. Slip stitch these edges together, working through back of knit stitches on rib so that joining seam does not show. Slide a piece of foam between the two soles and then use mattress stitch to sew them together.

For each slipper, cut 3 x 50cm (20in) lengths of A and twist together to make a cord. Knot ends together and trim close to knot. Sew centre of twisted cord to front of slipper to either left or right of cable and tie in a knot. With B, make 2 small pompons and sew securely to ends of twisted cord.

Textured scarves

A 'hairy' eyelash yarn makes a fun accessory from the simplest of stitches.

The eye-catching colourful yarn is the main feature of these simple garter-stitch scarves.

GETTING STARTED

 Worked throughout in basic garter stitch but knitting with eyelash yarn takes some practice

Size:
Long narrow scarf is approximately 10cm wide x 220cm (4in x 86in) long
Crossover scarf is approximately 14cm wide x 70cm (5½in x 27½in) long

How much yarn:
Stylecraft Milan, approx 35m (39 yards) per ball
Long narrow scarf: 3 x 50g (2oz) balls
Crossover scarf: 2 x 50g (2oz) balls

Needles:
Pair of 7.5mm (no. 11/US 10½) knitting needles

Additional items:
Large button for crossover scarf

Tension/gauge:
10 sts and approximately 16 rows measure 10cm (4in) square over g st on 7.5mm (no. 11 US 10½) needles

What you have to do:
Work throughout in garter stitch (every row knit) for both scarfs. For crossover scarf, make cast/bound-off buttonhole in centre of scarf close to one end. Sew on button after fitting round neck.

The Yarn
Stylecraft Milan is a 100% polyester speciality yarn with colourful slubs and distinctive long 'eyelash' fibres. It can be machine washed and there are plenty of attractive colourways to use with simple stitches to emphasize the 'hairy' quality of the yarn.

Abbreviations:
cm = centimetre(s);
cont = continue;
g st = garter stitch
(every row knit);
k = knit;
st(s) = stitch(es)

Instructions

LONG NARROW SCARF:

Cast on 10 sts. Work in g st until Scarf measures 220cm
(86in). Cast/bind off.

CROSSOVER SCARF:

Cast on 14 sts.
Work 10 rows in g st.
1st buttonhole row: K6, Cast/bind off next 2 sts, k to
end.
2nd buttonhole row: K to end, casting on 2 sts over
those cast/bound off in previous row.
Cont in g st until Scarf measures 70cm (27½in). Cast/bind
off.
Sew button to centre of Scarf 8cm (3in) down from cast/
bound-off edge, or in position required when wrapped
around neck.

HOW TO
WORK WITH EYELASH YARN

This yarn is knitted on fairly large needles to give the other elements – the eyelash strands and the small slubs – enough space when the stitches are formed to spread into an overall fabric.

1 Cast on in the usual way, making sure that the cast-on stitches are even and that they are not too tight around the right-hand needle.

2 Both scarfs are knitted in garter stitch. Work the rows of knit stitch keeping an even tension/gauge.

3 With an eyelash yarn like this, the most important rule for keeping your tension/gauge even is to make sure that the yarn can flow freely through your fingers as you knit. This may take a little practice as the yarn is not smooth.

4 The yarn knits up quickly, as it is worked on large needles. If you keep the tension/gauge even the fabric will have straight sides and the eyelash fibres will stand out from the main part of the fabric.

Shaker hearts

This collection of quick and easy hearts would make the perfect present for a new homeowner.

These stocking/stockinette-stitch hearts with decorative colour work and embroidery are just right to hang in your home.

GETTING STARTED

 Basic heart (red) is very easy to make but pink and white hearts involve some simple colourwork from charts

Size:
Each finished heart is approximately 11cm x 13cm (4¼in x 5in)

How much yarn:
1 x 50g (2oz) ball of Patons Diploma Gold DK, approx 120m (131 yards) per ball, in each of three colours A, B and C

Needles:
Pair of 4mm (no. 8/US 6) knitting needles

Additional items:
Polyester toy stuffing
5 small white buttons
1 large white button
75cm (30in) of narrow red satin ribbon
Sewing needle and thread

Tension/gauge:
22 sts and 28 rows measure 10cm (4in) square over st st on 4mm (no. 8/US 6) needles
IT IS ESSENTIAL TO WORK TO THE STATED TENSION/GAUGE TO ACHIEVE SUCCESS

What you have to do:
Work main fabric in stocking/stockinette stitch, shaping as instructed. Pink and white hearts involve colour work pattern with Fair Isle and intarsia techniques. Decorate hearts with simple embroidery or sew on buttons. Stitch in ribbon for hanging loop.

The Yarn
Patons Diploma Gold DK is a practical mixture of 55% wool, 25% acrylic and 20% nylon. There is a comprehensive shade range with plenty of choice for colour work.

 ## Instructions

Abbreviations:
beg = beginning; **cm** = centimetre(s);
cont = continue; **dec** = decrease(ing); **foll** = follows;
k = knit; **p** = purl; **rem** = remain; **rep** = repeat;
RS = right side; **st(s)** = stitch(es);
st st = stocking/stockinette stitch; **tog** = together;
WS = wrong side; **yfwd** = yarn forward/yarn over;
yrn = yarn round needle/yarn over

RED HEART
BACK:

With A, cast on 3 sts. Cont in st st and shape as foll:

1st row: P to end.

Next row: (RS) K1, (yfwd, k1) twice. 5 sts.

Next row: P1, yrn, p into back of loop made on previous row, p1, p into back of loop made on previous row, yrn, p1. 7 sts.

Next row: K1, yfwd, k into back of loop made on previous row, k to last 2 sts, k into back of loop made on previous row, yfwd, k1.

Next row: P1, yrn, p into back of loop made on previous row, p to last 2 sts, p into back of loop made on previous row, yrn, p1.

Rep last 2 rows until there are 31 sts. Work 19 rows straight, ending with a k row.

Shape top:

Next row: P16, turn and cont on these sts only.

Next row: Cast/bind off 1 st, k to last 2 sts, k2tog. 14 sts.

Dec 1 st at each end of next 4 rows. Cast/bind off rem 6 sts.

With WS facing, rejoin yarn to rem 15 sts and p to end.

Dec 1 st at beg of next row. 14 sts. Dec 1 st at each end of next 4 rows. Cast/bind off rem 6 sts.

FRONT:

Work as given for Back.

WHITE HEART
BACK:

With C, work as given for Red Heart.

FRONT:

With C, work as given for Back, placing small squares patt as shown on Chart 2. Use small, separate balls of C at either side of small squares patt, twisting yarns tog on WS of work when changing colours to avoid holes forming and strand A and B loosely across WS of work.

PINK HEART
BACK:

With B, work as given for Red heart.

FRONT:

With B, work as given for Back, placing gingham patt as shown on Chart 3. Strand colours not in use loosely across WS of work.

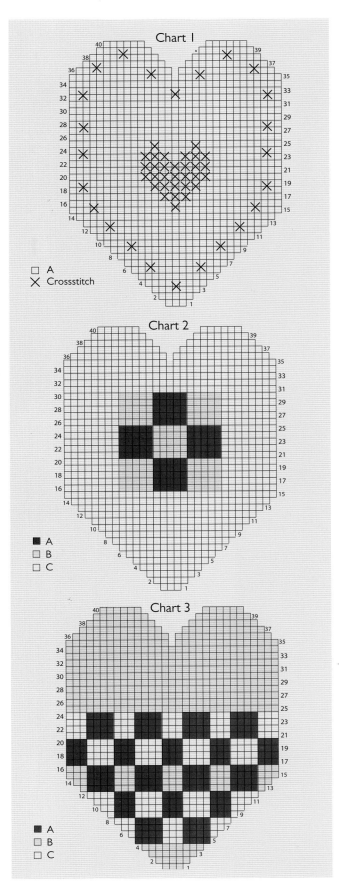

Chart 1

□ A
✕ Crossstitch

Chart 2

■ A
□ B
□ C

Chart 3

■ A
□ B
□ C

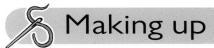 Making up

RED HEART:

With C and following Chart 1, work cross-stitch heart motif in centre of front and individual cross stitches for border. Cut a 25cm (10in) length of ribbon and fold in half to form a loop. With matching sewing thread stitch raw edges of ribbon loop securely to WS of top of front heart. With RS facing, backstitch around front and back, leaving a small opening in one side. Turn to RS through opening, stuff lightly and close opening.

WHITE HEART:

Sew a small white button to centre of each pink square. Cut a 25cm (10in) length of ribbon and fold in half to form a loop. With matching sewing thread stitch raw edges of ribbon loop securely to WS of top of front heart. With RS facing, backstitch around front and back, leaving a small opening in one side. Turn to RS through opening, stuff lightly and close opening.

PINK HEART:

Cut a 25cm (10in) length of ribbon and fold in half to form a loop. With matching sewing thread stitch raw edges of ribbon loop securely to WS of top of front heart. With RS facing, backstitch around front and back, leaving a small opening in one side. Turn to RS through opening, stuff lightly and close opening. Sew large white button to top centre front of heart.

Long cable socks

These socks are the perfect partner for
Ugg-style boots.

Hand-knitted on four needles in the traditional way, these socks have a long leg with cable trim and cuff that will peep out from the top of your boots.

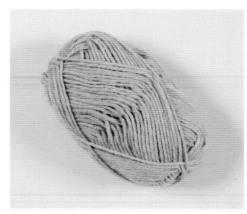

The Yarn

King Cole Merino DK contains 100% pure new wool in a machine-washable format that is perfect for socks. There are loads of great contemporary colours to choose from, as well as some more traditional ones.

GETTING STARTED

 Working in rounds on double-pointed needles requires practice, especially for socks that have a lot of shaping

Size:
To fit adult foot
Length from top to heel (with top turned over):
approximately 40cm (16in)
Length from heel to toe: *22cm (8½in) (adjustable)*
How much yarn:
5 x 50g (2oz) balls of King Cole Merino DK, approx 112m (123 yards) per ball
Needles:
Set of four double-pointed 3.25mm (no. 10/US 3) knitting needles
Cable needle
Tension/gauge:
24 sts and 32 rows measures 10cm (4in) square over st st on 3.25mm (no. 10/US 3) needles
IT IS ESSENTIAL TO WORK TO THE STATED TENSION/ GAUGE TO ACHIEVE SUCCESS
What you have to do:
Work main fabric in rounds of stocking/stockinette stitch with cable panel down outside of leg. Reverse fabric after working cuff. Use simple shaping for legs. Divide stitches for heel, working in rows. Pick up stitches down sides of heel for instep. Graft toe or Cast/bind off stitches together.

Abbreviations:

beg = beginning;
cm = centimetre(s);
cont = continue;
C6B(F) = cable 6 back(front) as foll: sl next 3 sts on to cable needle and leave at back(front) of work, k3, then k 3 sts from cable needle;
dec = decrease(ing);
foll = follows;
inc = increasing; **k** = knit;
p = purl; **patt** = pattern;
psso = pass slipped stitch over; **rem** = remain(ing);
rep = repeat; **sl** = slip;
st(s) = stitch(es);
st st = stocking/stockinette stitch; **tog** = together

Instructions

SOCK:

With set of 3.25mm (no. 10/US 3) double-pointed needles cast 70 sts as foll: 23 sts on to 1st and 2nd needles and 24 sts on to 3rd needle. Work 3 rounds in k1, p1 rib.

Border:

1st round: K11, p2, k9, p2, k22, p2, k9, p2, k11.
2nd round: As 1st round.
3rd round: K11, p2, C6F, k3, p2, k22, p2, C6F, k3, p2, k11.
4th–6th rounds: As 1st round.
7th round: K11, p2, k3, C6B, p2, k22, p2, k3, C6B, p2, k11.
8th round: As 1st round. Rep these 8 rounds twice more, dec 2 sts evenly on last round. 68 sts.
Next round: *K2, p2, rep from * to end.
Work 15 more rounds in k2, p2 rib, inc 2 sts evenly on last round. 70 sts. Turn work inside out to reverse fabric and cont in patt as foll:
41st and 42nd rounds: As 1st round.
43rd round: K11, p2, C6B, k3, p2, k22, p2, C6B, k3, p2, k11.
44th–46th rounds: As 1st round.
47th round: K11, p2, k3, C6F, p2, k22, p2, k3, C6F, zp2, k11.
48th round: As 1st round.
Cont in patt as set until sock measures 26cm (10¼in) from beg.

Shape leg:

** Next round: K1, sl 1, k1, psso, work to last 3 sts, k2tog, k1. Work 5 rounds straight.**
Rep from ** to ** 5 times more. 58 sts. Cont in patt until

work measures 39cm (15½in) from beg.

Divide for heel:

Patt 14 sts, sl last 15 sts of round on to other end of same needle (these 29 sts for heel). Divide rem sts on to two needles and leave for instep.

Heel:

Beg and ending with a p row, work 6cm (2½in) in st st.

Turn heel:

1st row: K18, sl 1, k1, psso, turn.
2nd row: P8, p2tog, turn.
3rd row: K8, sl 1, k1, psso, turn.
Rep 2nd and 3rd rows 8 times more, then work 2nd row again.
Next row: K5 to complete heel (4 sts rem unworked on left-hand needle).
Sl all instep sts on to one needle, k4 heel sts, pick up and k 16 sts along side of heel, using 2nd needle k across instep sts, using 3rd needle, pick up and k 16 sts along other side of heel, k5 heel sts. 70 sts.

Shape instep:

1st round: K to end.
2nd round: On 1st needle, k to last 3 sts, k2tog, k1; on 2nd needle, k to end; on 3rd needle, k1, sl 1, k1, psso, k to end.
Rep 1st and 2nd rounds until 56 sts rem.
Cont on these sts until foot measures 16cm (6¼in) or length required (less 6cm (2½in) for toe shaping). Sl 1 st from end of 2nd needle onto 1st needle.

Shape toe:

1st round: On 1st needle, k to last 3 sts, k2tog, k1; on 2nd needle, k1, sl 1, k1, psso, k to last 3 sts, k2tog, k1; on 3rd needle, k1, sl 1, k1, psso, k to end.

2nd and 3rd rounds: K to end.

Rep last 3 rounds until 32 sts rem, then k sts from 1st needle on to end of 3rd needle. Graft sts or cast/bind off sts from needles tog.

Intarsia scented sachet

This lavender sachet makes a perfect gift and it's a great way to practise your intarsia techniques.

Worked in double knitting (light worsted) yarn on smaller needles than recommended, the close stitches of this pretty flower-patterned sachet resemble an embroidered tapestry.

GETTING STARTED

 Although intarsia knitting is generally quite advanced, this is an ideal small-scale project for new-comers to the technique

Size:
Sachet is approximately 18cm x 18cm (7in x 7in)

How much yarn:
1 x 50g (2oz) ball of King Cole Merino DK, approx 112m (123 yards) per ball, in each of eight colours A, B, C, D, E, F, G and H

Needles:
Pair of 3.75mm (no. 9/US 5) knitting needles

Additional items:
Scented sachet approximately 18cm x 18cm (7in x 7in)

Tension/gauge:
23 sts and 30 rows measure 10cm (4in) square over st st on 3.75mm (no. 9/US 5) needles
IT IS ESSENTIAL TO WORK TO THE STATED TENSION/GAUGE TO ACHIEVE SUCCESS

What you have to do:
Work back of sachet in stocking/stockinette stitch in main colour only. Work front of sachet in stocking/stockinette stitch, following pattern from chart. Use intarsia techniques of small balls of yarn for separate areas of colour, twisting yarns together on wrong side when changing colour to prevent holes.

The Yarn
King Cole Merino DK contains 100% pure wool in a machine-washable format. There are plenty of shades to choose from for attractive colour work.

Abbreviations:
beg = beginning;
cm = centimetre(s);
cont = continue;
k = knit;
p = purl;
patt = pattern;
RS = right side;
st(s) = stitch(es);
st st = stocking/
stockinette stitch;
tog = together;
WS = wrong side

 # Instructions

BACK:

With A, cast on 43 sts. Beg with a k row, cont in st st and work 52 rows, ending with a p row. Cast/bind off.

FRONT:

With A, cast on 43 sts. Beg with a k row, cont in st st and patt from chart, reading odd-numbered (k) rows from right to left and even-numbered (p) rows from left to right. Use small separate balls of yarn for each area of colour and twist yarns tog on WS of work when changing colour to avoid holes forming. When 52 rows from chart have been completed, cast/bind off.

 # Making up

Darn in ends of yarn carefully on WS of work. Press pieces carefully according to directions on ball band. With RS of Back and Front facing, backstitch around three sides, leaving one side of sachet open. Turn sachet RS out. Insert scented sachet (if you are unable to find one the correct size, then sew a sachet from cotton lining fabric and fill it with dried, scented flowers) and neatly slip stitch open side closed.

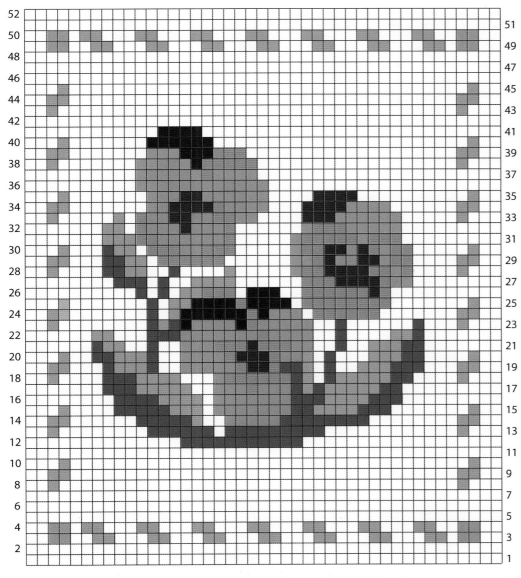

□	A
■	B
■	C
■	D
■	E
■	F
■	G
■	H

Textured beret

The snug-fitting ribbed band means that this beret can be pulled into all kinds of different shapes on your head.

With its deep ribbed band and generous textured crown, this beret is right on trend.

GETTING STARTED

Easy stitches and shaping make this an ideal design for a beginner

Size:

To fit woman's head: small[medium:large]

Note: *Figures in square brackets [ ] refer to larger sizes; where there is only one set of figures, it applies to all sizes*

How much yarn:

2 x 50g (2oz) balls of Debbie Bliss Rialto Aran, approx 80m (87 yards) per ball

Needles:

Pair of 4mm (no. 8/US 6) knitting needles
Pair of 5mm (no. 6/US 8) knitting needles

Additional items:

Stitch markers

Tension/gauge:

20 sts and 28 rows measure 10cm (4in) square over stocking/stockinette stitch on 5mm (no. 6/US 8) needles
IT IS ESSENTIAL TO WORK TO THE STATED TENSION/ GAUGE TO ACHIEVE SUCCESS

What you have to do:

Work band in double (k2, p2) rib. Work main part in double moss/seed stitch. Insert markers to denote shaping positions for crown. Shape crown by knitting two stitches together at marked positions, and working pattern elsewhere.

The Yarn

Debbie Bliss Rialto Aran contains 100% merino wool. Its slight twist gives good stitch definition for textured patterns and it can be machine washed at a low temperature. There are plenty of contemporary colours to choose from.

Abbreviations:

alt = alternate;
beg = beginning;
cm = centimetre(s);
cont = continue;
dec = decrease;
foll = follows;
inc = increase(ing);
k = knit;
m1 = make one stitch by picking up strand lying between needles and knitting into back of it;
p = purl;
patt = pattern;
rem = remain(ing);
rep = repeat;
RS = right side;
st(s) = stitch(es);
tog = together;
WS = wrong side

Instructions

BERET:
With 4mm (no. 8/US 6) needles cast on 86[94:102] sts.
1st row: (RS) *K2, p2, rep from * to last 2 sts, k2.
2nd row: *P2, k2, rep from * to last 2 sts, p2.
Rep these 2 rows to form rib for 5cm (2in), ending with a WS row.
1st size only:
Inc row: (K1, m1) twice, *m1, p2, m1, k2, rep from * to end. 130 sts.
2nd size only:
Inc row: K2, *m1, p2, m1, k2, rep from * to end. 140 sts.
3rd size only:
Inc row: K2, p2, *m1, k2, m1, p2, rep from * to last 2 sts, k2. 150 sts.

All sizes:
Cont in double moss/seed st as foll:
1st and 2nd rows: *K1, p1, rep from * to end.
3rd and 4th rows: *P1, k1, rep from * to end.
These 4 rows form patt. Cont in patt until work measures 13cm (5in) from beg, ending with a WS row.
Shape crown:
Dec row: Patt 11[12:13], k2tog, insert marker, rep from * 9 times more.
Next row: *P1, patt 11[12:13], rep from * 9 times more.
Next row: *Patt 10[11:12], k2tog, rep from * 9 times more.
Next row: *P1, patt 10[11:12], rep from * 9 times more.

Cont to dec as set, working k2tog before each marker on next and every alt row and in patt between, until 20 sts rem, ending with a WS row.

Next row: *K2tog, rep from * to end. 10 sts.
Cut off yarn. Thread cut end through rem sts, pull up tightly and secure. Join back seam.

HOW TO
WORK THE PATTERN

1 Cast on the instructed number of stitches and work in knit two, purl two rib until the fabric measures 5cm (2in).

3 Begin the double moss/seed stitch pattern by working a sequence of knit one and purl one to the end of the row. Repeat this for the second row.

2 Increase in the next rib row by making stitches as instructed. To make a stitch, place the tip of the right-hand needle under the horizontal strand between the stitch on the right-hand needle and the next stitch on the left-hand needle and knit as if it were a regular stitch.

4 On the third and fourth rows, work a sequence of purl one and knit one to the end of each row. These four rows form the pattern and are repeated as instructed.

Giant key tassel

Attach this tassel to a key to make a decorative addition to any set of drawers or door.

This giant tassel, embellished with beads and sequins, uses the general principles of tassel making along with some simple crochet.

The Yarn

Debbie Bliss Prima contains 80% bamboo and 20% merino wool. It has a slightly silky finish and the colours have a subtle sheen that complements the softly spun appearance and variegated colouring of Debbie Bliss SoHo, containing 100% handspun wool slub.

GETTING STARTED

 Tassels are easy to make but you will need a few basic crochet and sewing stitches for decoration

Size:
Tassel is approximately 15cm long (excluding chain loop) x 3.5cm wide (6in x 1½in)

How much yarn:
1 x 50g (2oz) ball of Debbie Bliss Prima, approx 100m (109 yards) per ball, in each of two colours A and B
1 x 50g (2oz) ball of Debbie Bliss SoHo, approx 66m (72 yards) per ball in C

Additional items:
3.5mm (UK 9/US 4/E) crochet hook, thick card

Round sequins in pink and gold
Seed beads in pink, gold and yellow
Tapestry needle, sewing needle and thread

What you have to do:
Add sequins to six lengths of smooth yarn, working crochet chain stitches between each one. Form tassel by winding all yarns together around length of card, adding sequinned lengths last. Secure yarns at top of card, then cut through yarns at lower edge. Wind yarn around top of tassel to form 'head' and decorate with beads and fancy stitches. Work chain ties with long lengths of yarn left at top of tassel.

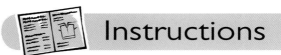

Instructions

Abbreviations:
ch = chain; **cm** = centimetre(s); **rep** = repeat; **st(s)** = stitch(es)

TASSEL:
Sequinned lengths:
Note: You may find threading sequins easier with a sewing needle and thread.

With 3.5mm (UK 9/US 4/E) crochet hook and A, start with a slip knot, then make 2ch, *slide a pink sequin along yarn until it rests against last ch worked, make 2ch, rep from * until 10 sequins have been secured, work approximately 14cm (5½in) in ch, **add sequin, make 2ch, rep from ** until 10 more sequins have been secured. Fasten off.

Make another two lengths using A and pink sequins, then make three lengths using B and gold sequins. Leave sequinned lengths on one side.

Making tassel:
Cut a piece of card measuring 16cm (6¼in) long × approximately 5cm (2in) wide. Then holding yarns A, B

and C together, wrap around card lengthwise until it is thickly and evenly covered.

Now, lay sequinned sections over wrapped card so that chain section in middle of each one lays over top sections of yarns and card and an even length of sequins and chain hangs down on either side.

Take a length of A and pass it under all of yarns at very top of card and tie tightly to secure, then cut off leaving long ends.

Carefully cut all yarns at opposite end (bottom) of card, taking care not to cut sequinned chain sections, and remove card.

Approximately 3cm (1¼in) down from top of tassel, wrap B three times around all threads. Tie yarn to secure, then thread through a tapestry needle and use this to sew through all yarns to other side of tassel. Then sew vertical sts over the wrapped yarn B at regular intervals all around tassel. Repeat this process working down the tassel with yarn C and then yarn A.

Sew seed beads either side of each vertical st on wrapped section, using sewing thread and pink beads on section in A and yellow and gold beads on section in B.

With 3.5mm (UK 9/US 4/E) crochet hook and long lengths of A at top of tassel, work in ch for approximately 10cm (4in) (or length required). Fasten off.

With tapestry needle and B, sew over yarns at top of tassel in a lattice pattern.

Trim all yarns at lower edge of tassel to an even length. Use ch sections at top of tassel to attach it to your key.

Multi-coloured gloves

Pick different colours for fingers and thumbs to make these distinctive gloves.

When it's cold enough for gloves, then these funky stocking/stockinette stitch ones with different-coloured fingers and striped cuffs are great fun to wear.

The Yarn

Debbie Bliss Cashmerino DK is a blend of 55% merino wool with 33% microfibre and 12% cashmere. It produces a luxuriously soft fabric that can be machine washed at a low temperature and there are plenty of contemporary colours to choose from.

GETTING STARTED

 Although the fabric is a basic one, the construction of gloves is not straightforward

Size:

To fit an average woman's hand

How much yarn:

1 x 50g (2oz) ball of Debbie Bliss Cashmerino DK, approx 110m (120 yards) per ball, in each of following six colours A, B, C, D, E and F

Needles:

Pair of 3.25mm (no. 10/US 3) knitting needles
Pair of 3.75mm (no. 9/US 5) knitting needles

Additional items:

Stitch holder

Tension/gauge:

23 sts and 32 rows measure 10cm (4in) square over st st on 3.75mm (no. 9/US 5) needles
IT IS ESSENTIAL TO WORK TO THE STATED TENSION/GAUGE TO ACHIEVE SUCCESS

What you have to do:

Work cuffs in single (k1, p1) rib using stripes of all the colours. Work main part of gloves in stocking/stockinette stitch, increasing within fabric for thumb gusset. Shape thumb, then continue on main part of hand before working each finger individually in a different colour. Join seams on thumb and fingers as you are working, then join fourth finger and side seams afterwards.

Instructions

RIGHT GLOVE:

With 3.25mm (no. 10/US 3) needles and B, cast on 41 sts.

1st row: (RS) K1, *p1, k1, rep from * to end.

2nd row: P1, *k1, p1, rep from * to end.

These 2 rows form rib. Joining in and cutting off colours as required, work a further 8 rows in rib, working 2 rows each in C, D, E and F. Join in A and work a further 12 rows in rib, ending with a WS row.

Change to 3.75mm (no. 9/US 5) needles. Beg with a k row, cont in st st and work 6 rows.**

Shape thumb gusset:

Next row: (RS) K21, m1, k3, m1, k17. 43 sts.

Work 3 rows in st st.

Next row: K21, m1, k5, m1, k17. 45 sts.

Work 3 rows in st st.

Next row: K21, m1, k7, m1, k17. 47 sts.

Work 3 rows in st st.

Next row: K21, m1, k9, m1, k17. 49 sts.

Work 3 rows in st st.

Next row: K21, m1, k11, m1, k17. 51 sts.

Work 3 rows in st st, ending with a WS row.

Shape thumb:

Next row: (RS) K21 A, join in B and k13 B, turn and cast on 2 sts.

Next row: P15 B, turn and cast on 2 sts.

*** Cont in B on these 17 sts and work 14 rows, ending with a WS row.

Next row: K2, k2tog, (k3, k2tog) twice, k3. 14 sts.

Next row: P to end.

Next row: (K2tog) 7 times.

Cut off yarn. Thread through rem 7 sts, pull up tightly and fasten off securely. Join thumb seam.

With RS of work facing, join in A and pick up and k 5 sts from base of thumb, k to end. 43 sts.

Cont in A and work 11 rows, ending with a WS row.

Cut off A.

Shape first finger:

With RS of work facing, sl first 15 sts on to a holder and join in C.

Next row: (RS) K13 C, turn and cast on 1 st.

Next row: P14 C, turn and cast on 1 st.

Cont in C on these 15 sts and work 20 rows, ending with a WS row.

Next row: K1, k2tog, (k3, k2tog) twice, k2. 12 sts.

Next row: P to end.

Next row: (K2tog) 6 times.

Cut off yarn. Thread through rem 6 sts, pull up tightly and fasten off securely. Join finger seam.

Shape fourth finger:
With RS of work facing, join in F and pick up and k 3 sts from base of third finger, k5.
Next row: (WS) P13 F.
Cont in F on these 13 sts and work 16 rows, ending with a WS row.
Next row: K1, (k2tog, k2) 3 times. 10 sts.
Next row: P to end.
Next row: (K2tog) 5 times.
Cut off yarn. Thread through rem 5 sts, pull up tightly and fasten off securely.

LEFT GLOVE:
Work as given for Right glove to **.
Shape thumb gusset:
Next row: (RS) K17, m1, k3, m1, k21. 43 sts.
Work 3 rows in st st.
Next row: K17, m1, k5, m1, k21. 45 sts.
Work 3 rows in st st.
Next row: K17, m1, k7, m1, k21. 47 sts.
Work 3 rows in st st.
Next row: K17, m1, k9, m1, k21. 49 sts.
Work 3 rows in st st.
Next row: K17, m1, k11, m1, k21. 51 sts.
Work 3 rows in st st, ending with a WS row.
Shape thumb:
Next row: (RS) K17 A, join in B and k13 B, turn and cast on 2 sts.
Next row: P15 B, turn and cast on 2 sts.
Complete as given for Right glove from *** to end.

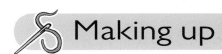

Making up

Press according to directions on ball band. Join fourth finger and side seams.

Shape second finger:
With RS of work facing, join in D and pick up and k 3 sts from base of first finger, k5, turn and cast on 1 st.
Next row: (WS) P14 D, turn and cast on 1 st.
Cont in D on these 15 sts and work 22 rows, ending with a WS row.
Next row: K1, k2tog, (k3, k2tog) twice, k2. 12 sts.
Next row: P to end.
Next row: (K2tog) 6 times.
Cut off yarn. Thread through rem 6 sts, pull up tightly and fasten off securely. Join finger seam.
Shape third finger:
With RS of work facing, join in E and pick up and k 3 sts from base of second finger, k5, turn and cast on 1 st.
Next row: (WS) P14 E, turn and cast on 1 st.
Cont in E on these 15 sts and work 20 rows, ending with a WS row.
Next row: K1, k2tog, (k3, k2tog) twice, k2. 12 sts.
Next row: P to end.
Next row: (K2tog) 6 times.
Cut off yarn. Thread through rem 6 sts, pull up tightly and fasten off securely. Join finger seam.

Diamond and rib book cover

Wrap your favourite sketchbook or notebook in this distinctive cabled jacket.

Worked from flap to flap in hardwearing cotton, this book cover is highly patterned with side panels and textured diamonds. Keep your book closed with two plaited/braided ties.

GETTING STARTED

 Straight strip of fabric but pattern is quite complicated and requires attention

Size:
To fit a standard A4 (8½in x 11in) hardback sketch or note book
Cover is 69cm long x 30cm wide (27in x 12in), before making up

How much yarn:
2 x 100g (3½oz) balls of Patons 100% Cotton DK, approx 210m (230 yards) per ball

Needles:
Pair of 4mm (no. 8/US 6) knitting needles

Tension/gauge:
22 sts and 28 rows measure 10cm (4in) square over st st on 4mm (no. 8/US 6) needles
IT IS ESSENTIAL TO WORK TO THE STATED TENSION/GAUGE TO ACHIEVE SUCCESS

What you have to do:
Start working first flap in stocking/stockinette stitch with rib edging. Continue in main fabric – double moss/seed stitch and diamond cable panels. End with second flap worked in same way as first. Make two plaited/braided cord ties.

The Yarn
Patons 100% Cotton DK is a pure cotton yarn with a slight twist. It is ideal for textured stitch patterns, can be machine washed and there are plenty of interesting colours to choose from.

Abbreviations:

beg = beginning;
cm = centimetre(s);
cont = continue;
foll = follow(s)(ing);
k = knit;
m1 = make one stitch by picking up strand lying between needles and purling into back of it;
p = purl;
patt = pattern;
rep = repeat;
RS = right side;
st(s) = stitch(es);
st st = stocking/stockinette stitch;
tw2 = knit into front of 2nd stitch on left needle, then knit first stitch and slip both stitches off needle together;
WS = wrong side

Instructions

PATTERN PANEL 1:
(Worked over 6 sts)
1st row: (RS) K2, p2, tw2.
2nd row: P2, k2, p2.
3rd–12th rows: Rep 1st and 2nd rows 5 times.
13th row: Tw2, p2, k2.
14th row: As 2nd row.
15th–24th rows: Rep 13th and 14th rows 5 times.
Rep these 24 rows to form patt.

PATTERN PANEL 2:
(Worked over 19 sts)
1st row: (RS) P8, k3, p8.
2nd and every foll WS row: K the k sts and p the p sts.
3rd row: P7, k5, p7.
5th row: P6, k3, p1, k3, p6.
7th row: P5, k3, p1, k1, p1, k3, p5.
9th row: P4, k3, p1, (k1, p1) twice, k3, p4.
11th row: P3, k3, p1, (k1, p1) 3 times, k3, p3.

13th row: P2, k3, p1, (k1, p1) 4 times, k3, p2.
15th row: As 11th row.
17th row: As 9th row.
19th row: As 7th row.
21st row: As 5th row.
23rd row: As 3rd row.
24th row: As 2nd row.
Rep these 24 rows to form patt.

BOOK COVER:
First flap:
Cast on 68 sts. Work 4 rows in k1, p1 rib. Beg with a k row, cont in st st until flap measures 13cm (5in), ending with a k row.
Inc row: (WS) P7, m1, (p6, m1) 9 times, p7. 78 sts.
Front:
Cont in patt as foll:
1st row: (P1, k1) 5 times, p1, work next 6 sts as 1st row of Pattern Panel 1, (work next 19 sts as 1st row of Pattern Panel 2, work next 6 sts as 1st row of Pattern Panel 1) twice, p1, (k1, p1) 5 times.

2nd row: (K1, p1) 5 times, k1, work next 6 sts as 2nd row of Pattern Panel 1, (work next 19 sts as 2nd row of Pattern Panel 2, work next 6 sts as 2nd row of Pattern Panel 1) twice, k1, (p1, k1) 5 times.

3rd row: (K1, p1) 5 times, p1, work next 6 sts as 3rd row of Pattern Panel 1, (work next 19 sts as 3rd row of Pattern Panel 2, work next 6 sts as 3rd row of Pattern Panel 1) twice, p1 (p1, k1) 5 times.

4th row: (P1, k1) 5 times, k1, work next 6 sts as 4th row of Pattern Panel 1, (work next 19 sts as 4th row of Pattern Panel 2, work next 6 sts as 4th row of Pattern Panel 1) twice, k1, (k1, p1) 5 times.

Cont in patt as set until 24 rows of both patt panels have been worked 5 times.

Next row: (RS) (P1, k1) 5 times, p1, k2, p2, k2, (work next 19 sts as 1st row of Pattern Panel 1, k2, p2, k2) twice, p1, (k1, p1) 5 times.

Dec row: (WS) P7, (p2tog, p5) 10 times, p1. 68 sts.

Second flap:
Beg with a k row, cont in st st until flap measures 12cm (5in), ending with a p row. Work 4 rows in k1, p1 rib. Cast/bind off in rib.

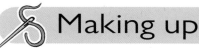

Making up

Fold flaps over so that RS are together and stitch to front and back along side edges. Turn RS out.

For each tie, cut three 70cm (27½in) lengths of yarn. Thread one length through each of 3 stitches on last row of diamond pattern before flap. Pull through so that they are same length. Using in pairs, plait/braid together until tie is 20cm (8in) long. Tie a knot and then trim ends. Insert book and tie to close.

Pompom doorstop

Prop your door ajar with this weighty doorstop topped with a useful loop for lifting and decorative pompoms.

Stop the door slamming shut with this weighted container covered with a striped stocking/stockinette stitch cover, gathered at the top with pompom-trimmed drawstring and incorporating a useful ring for lifting.

GETTING STARTED

Knitted cover is easy to make but pay attention to preparing base of doorstop correctly

Size:
Doorstop is approximately 15cm diameter x 23cm high (6in x 9in)

How much yarn:
1 x 50g (2oz) ball of Sirdar Peru, approx 90m (99 yards) per ball, in each of three colours A, B and C

Needles:
Pair of 6.5mm (no. 3/US 10½) knitting needles
Pair of 6.5mm (no. 3/US 10½) double-pointed knitting needles

Additional items:
Cylindrical plastic container with screw top measuring about 11cm in diameter x 15cm high x 35cm in circumference (4½in x 6in x 13¾in)
Rice, sand or dried pulses to fill container
Wadding/batting for sides and top of container
Button, medium size with 4 holes
Wire or memory thread
Wooden curtain ring, 5.5cm (approx 2in) in diameter
Tapestry needle

Tension/gauge:
14 sts and 19 rows measure 10cm (4in) square over st st on 6.5mm (no. 3/US 10½) needles
IT IS ESSENTIAL TO WORK TO THE STATED TENSION/ GAUGE TO ACHIEVE SUCCESS

What you have to do:
Make cover for container in striped stocking/stockinette stitch with simple shaping for circular base piece. Knit an i-cord drawstring and make pompoms to trim. Follow instructions to prepare container, including wiring on curtain ring for loop at top of doorstop. Weight container, cover with wadding/batting and add knitted outer layer.

The Yarn
Sirdar Peru is a chunky weight yarn containing 50% wool, 40% acrylic and 10% alpaca. It produces a homespun natural fabric and there is a small range of natural and subtle colours to choose from with a slight tweedy appearance.

Abbreviations:

beg = beginning;
cm = centimetre(s);
cont = continue; **k** = knit;
m1 = make one stitch by picking up strand lying between needles and working into back of it;
p = purl;
psso = pass slipped stitch over;
rep = repeat;
RS = right side; **sl** = slip;
st(s) = stitch(es);
st st = stocking/ stockinette stitch;
tbl = through back of loops;
tog = together;
yfwd = yarn forward/yarn over to make a stitch

Instructions

BASE:

With 6.5mm (no. 3/US 10½) needles and A, cast on 12 sts.
Beg with a k row, work 2 rows in st st.
Next row: K1, m1, k to last st, m1, k1.
P 1 row. Rep last 2 rows twice more. 18 sts. Beg with a k row, work 10 rows in st st.
Next row: Sl 1, k1, psso, k to last 2 sts, k2tog.
P 1 row. Rep last 2 rows twice more. 12 sts. Cast/bind off.

SIDE PIECE:

With 6.5mm (no. 3/US 10½) needles and A, cast on 56 sts.
Beg with a k row, cont in st st and stripe sequence of 4 rows each A, B and C.
Cont in stripes as set until work measures 21cm (8¼in) from beg, ending with 4th

row of stripe in A. Change to B.
Next row: (K1, k2tog) to last 2 sts, k2. 38 sts. P 1 row.
Next row: K2, (yfwd, k2tog, k2) to end. P 1 row. Change to C.
Next row: (K1, p1) to end.
Next row: (P1, k1) to end.
These 2 rows form moss/seed st. Rep them once more.
Cast/bind off in moss/seed st.

CORD:

With 6.5mm (no. 3/US 10½in) double-pointed needles and B, cast on 3 sts. K 1 row.
Next row: * Without turning work and RS facing, slide sts to other end of needle and, pulling yarn from left-hand side of sts to right across back, k1 tbl, k2. *
Rep from * to *, remembering to pull yarn tightly across back and always working a k row, until cord measures 40cm (16in). Cast/bind off.

CURTAIN RING COVER:

With 6.5mm (no. 3/US 10½in) needles and A, cast on 4 sts.
Beg with a k row, work 2 rows in st st.
Next row: K3, turn.
Next row: P2, turn.
Next row: K to end.
Next row: P to end.
Rep last 4 rows 7 times more or until cover fits around curtain ring. Cast/bind off.

 ## Making up

Remove any contents and stickers from container.
Thread 4-hole button with two lengths of wire or
memory thread and twist tog behind to secure. Make a
small hole in centre of container lid and thread twisted
wire through hole from underside and pull up so that
button sits against underside of lid. Fill container with rice,
sand or dried pulses so that it is heavy and screw lid back
on securely.

Cut a strip of wadding/batting to fit around sides of
container, and two circles of wadding/batting for the top
and bottom. Stick wadding/batting in place, making a hole
in centre of top circle for wire to pass through.

Join row ends of knitted side piece to form a tube, then
join in knitted base. Insert wadding/batting-covered
container into knitted container. Thread knitted cord
through eyelets at top of side piece, bringing both ends
out of last hole, and pull up slightly to gather, then wrap
ends of wire around and through curtain ring so that
ring sits just in top of gathered-up side piece. Twist wire
securely so that doorstop can be lifted up by curtain ring.

Sew cover over curtain ring with cast-on and cast/bound-
off edges at bottom next to wire. Swiss darn over any
holes in curtain ring cover if necessary.

Draw up knitted cord and knot to secure. Make two
pompoms with C and sew one to each end of cord.

Bright Aran cushion

Choose a bright colour to give a contemporary twist to a classic pattern.

Packed full of complex Aran textures, this beautiful cushion/pillow has all the traditional styling along with contemporary strong, bright colouring.

GETTING STARTED

Combination of complex cable panels is a challenge for an experienced knitter

Size:
Cushion/pillow is 40cm x 40cm (16in x 16in)

How much yarn:
6 x 50g (2oz) balls of Debbie Bliss Rialto Aran, approx 80m (87 yards) per ball

Needles:
Pair of 4.5mm (no. 7/US 7) knitting needles
Cable needle

Additional items:
40cm (16in) square cushion pad/pillow form

Tension/gauge:
20 sts and 28 rows measure 10cm (4in) square over double moss/seed st on 4.5mm (no. 7/US 7) needles
IT IS ESSENTIAL TO WORK TO THE STATED TENSION/ GAUGE TO ACHIEVE SUCCESS

What you have to do:
Work front in combination of cable panels with double moss/seed stitch at side edges. Work back entirely in double moss/seed stitch. Join three sides of back and front, insert cushion pad/pillow form and sew remaining side closed.

The Yarn
Debbie Bliss Rialto Aran contains 100% merino wool. The yarn produces clear stitch definition which is ideal for textured patterns and can be machine washed at a low temperature. There is a large palette of subtle and strong colours to choose from.

Abbreviations:

cm = centimetre(s);

cn = cable needle;

cont = continue;

foll = follow(s)(ing);

k = knit;

p = purl; **patt** = pattern;

rep = repeat;

RS = right side; **sl** = slip;

st(s) = stitch(es);

tog = together;

WS = wrong side

C3B = sl next st on to cn
and hold at back of work,
k2, then k st on cn

C3F = sl next 2 sts on
to cn and hold at front of
work, k1, then k 2 sts on cn

C3BP = sl next st on to
cn and hold at back of
work, k2, then p st on cn

C3FP = sl next 2 sts on
to cn and hold at front of
work, p1, then k 2 sts on cn

C4F = sl next 2 sts on
to cn and hold at front of
work, k2, then k 2 sts on cn

C5B = sl next 3 sts on
to cn and hold at back
of work, k2, sl p st from
cn back on to left-hand
needle, p this st, then k 2
sts on cn

C5F = sl next 3 sts on
to cn and hold at front of
work, k2, then sl p st from
cn back on to left-hand
needle, p this st, then k 2
sts on cn

MB = make bobble as foll:
(k1, p1, k1) all into next
st, turn and p3, turn and
k3tog

Instructions

BRAMBLE STITCH:
(Worked over 16 sts)
1st row: (RS) P16.
2nd row: K2, (p3tog, k1, p1, k1 all into next st) 3 times, k2.
3rd row: P16.
4th row: K2, (k1, p1, k1 all into next st, p3tog) 3 times, k2.
Rep these 4 rows to form patt.

OXO CABLE:
(Worked over 6 sts)
1st row: (RS) K6.
2nd and every foll WS row: P6.
3rd row: C3B, C3F.
5th row: K6.
7th row: C3F, C3B.
8th row: P6.
Rep these 8 rows to form patt.

SIMPLE CABLE:
(worked over 4 sts)
1st row: (RS) K4.

2nd row: P4.
3rd row: C4F.
4th row: P4.
Rep these 4 rows to form patt.

DIAMOND CABLE:
(Worked over 17 sts)
1st row: (RS) P6, k2, MB, k2, p6.
2nd and every foll WS row: K the k sts and p the p sts.
3rd row: P6, MB, k3, MB, p6.
5th row: As 1st row.
7th row: P5, C3BP, k1, C3FP, p5.
9th row: P4, C3BP, k1, p1, k1, C3FP, p4.
11th row: P3, C3BP, k1, (p1, k1) twice, C3FP, p3.
13th row: P2, C3BP, k1, (p1, k1) 3 times, C3FP, p2.
15th row: P2, C3FP, p1, (k1, p1) 3 times, C3BP, p2.
17th row: P3, C3FP, p1 (k1, p1) twice, C3BP, p3.
19th row: P4, C3FP, p1, k1, p1, C3BP, p4.

21st row: P5, C3FP, p1, C3BP, p5.
22nd row: K6, p5, k6.
Rep these 22 rows to form patt.

PLAITED/BRAIDED CABLE:
(Worked over 14 sts)
1st row: (RS) (K2, p1) 4 times, k2.
2nd and every foll WS row: (P2, k1) 4 times, p2.
3rd row: K2, (p1, C5F) twice.
5th and 7th rows: As 1st row.
9th row: (C5B, p1) twice, k2.
11th row: As 1st row.
12th row: As 2nd row.
Rep these 12 rows to form patt.

FRONT:
With 4.5mm (no. 7/US 7) needles cast on 104 sts.
Foundation row: (WS):*K2, (k1, p1, k1 all into next st, p3tog) 3 times*, k2, p6, k2, p4, k6, p5, k6, (p2, k1) 4 times, p2, k6, p5, k6, p4, k2, p6, rep from * to *, k2.
Now cont in patt as foll:
1st row: (RS) Work 16 sts as 1st row of Bramble stitch, work 6 sts at 1st row of Oxo cable, p2, work 4 sts as 1st row of Simple cable, work 17 sts as 1st row of Diamond cable, work 14 sts as 1st row of Plaited/braided cable, work 17 sts as 1st row of Diamond cable, work 4 sts as 1st row of Simple cable, p2, work 6 sts as 1st row of Oxo cable, work last 16 sts as 1st row of Bramble stitch.
2nd row: Work 16 sts as 2nd row of Bramble stitch, work 6 sts as 2nd row of Oxo cable, p2, work 4 sts as 2nd row of Simple cable, work 17 sts as 2nd row of Diamond cable, work 14 sts as 2nd row of Plaited/braided cable, work 17 sts as 2nd row of Diamond cable, work 4 sts as 2nd row of Simple cable, p2, work 6 sts as 2nd row of Oxo cable, work last 16 sts as 2nd row of Bramble stitch.
Cont in patt as now set until 22 rows of Diamond cable have been worked 5 times, then work a further 6 rows in patt. Cast/bind off.

BACK:
With 4.5mm (no. 7/US 7) needles cast on 81 sts. Cont in double moss/seed st as foll:
1st row: (RS) K1, *p1, k1, rep from * to end.
2nd row: P1, *k1, p1, rep from * to end.
3rd row: P1, *k1, p1, rep from * to end.
4th row: K1, *p1, k1, rep from * to end.

Rep these 4 rows until Back measures same as Front, ending with a WS row. Cast/bind off.

Making up

With RS together, join cast/bound-off edges (top) and side seams, leaving lower edge open. Turn RS out. Insert cushion pad/pillow form and use mattress stitch to close lower edge.

Party cakes

These scrumptious-looking cakes will brighten up any table!

Use double knitting (light worsted) yarn, mainly stocking/stockinette stitch and simple shaping for a selection of knitted cakes to whet your appetite.

The Yarn
Patons Diploma Gold DK is a practical mixture of 55% wool, 25% acrylic and 20% nylon. The wool-rich content of the yarn produces a good-looking fabric and there are plenty of fabulous colours to choose from.

GETTING STARTED

Easy pieces to knit but take care with details and construction for a good finished appearance

Size:
Chocolate cup cake: 6cm in diameter x 8cm high (2½in x 3in); Lemon cup cake: 6cm in diameter x 7cm high (2½in x 2¾in); Carrot cake: 8 x 9cm (3in x 3½in); Birthday cake: 10cm long x 6cm deep (4in x 2½in); Swiss rolls: 7cm in diameter x 2.5cm deep (2¾in x 1in)

How much yarn:
1 x 50g (2oz) ball of Patons Diploma Gold DK, approx 120m(131 yards) per ball, in each of six colours A – blue, B – chestnut, C – white, D – iris, E – lemon and F – ginger
Scraps of mohair yarn in two colours G – bright pink and H – white
Scraps of DK yarn in two colours I – pale orange and J – pale pink

Needles:
Pair of 3.75mm (no. 9/US 5) knitting needles

Additional items:
Washable polyester toy filling
Oddment of lightweight polyester wadding/batting
Small glass bead

Tension/gauge:
26 sts and 32 rows measure 10cm (4in) square over st st on 3.75mm (no. 9/US 5) needles
IT IS ESSENTIAL TO WORK TO THE STATED TENSION/ GAUGE TO ACHIEVE SUCCESS

What you have to do:
Work in stocking/stockinette stitch and reverse stocking/stockinette stitch. Follow instructions for simple increasing or decreasing to shape cakes. Make bobbles for iced decorations. Embellish carrot cake with French knots for carrots.

Abbreviations:

alt = alternate;
beg = beginning;
cm = centimetre(s);
cont = continue;
dec = decrease(ing);
foll = follow(s)(ing);
k = knit;
mb = make bobble as foll:
with colour K, work k1, p1,
k1, p1, k1 all into next st,
turn and beg with a p row,
work 4 rows st st on these
5 sts, then pass 4th, 3rd,
2nd and 1st st over 5th
st so that one st rem, slip
this st back on to left-hand
needle and k with C;
p = purl;
rem = remain(ing);
rep = repeat;
reverse st st = reverse
stocking/stockinette stitch
(purl side is right side);
RS = right side;
st(s) = stitch(es);
st st = stocking/
stockinette stitch;

Instructions

CHOCOLATE CUP CAKE:
Base:
With A, cast on 6 sts.
1st row: (RS) K1, k into front and back of next 5 sts.
11 sts.
2nd and foll alt rows: P to end.
3rd row: K into front and back of each st to end. 22 sts.
5th row: (K2, k into front and back of next st) 7 times, k1. 29 sts.
7th row: P to end.
Sides:
1st row: (WS) K1, (p1, k1) to end.
2nd row: P1, (k1, p1) to end.
3rd and 4th rows: As 1st and 2nd rows.
5th row: (K1, p1, k into front and back of next st, p1)
7 times, k1. 36 sts.

6th row: (P1, k1, p2, k1) to last st, p1.
7th–10th rows: Work 4 more rows in rib as set.
11th row: K to end. *
Top:
Change to B. Beg with a k row, work 6 rows in st st. Change to C and work 2 more rows.
Shape top:
1st row: (K4, k2tog) 6 times.
2nd and foll alt rows: P to end.
3rd row: (K3, k2tog) 6 times.
5th row: (K2, k2tog) 6 times.
7th row: (K1, k2tog) 6 times.
9th row: (K2tog) 6 times.
Cut off yarn. Thread cut end through rem sts, draw up tightly and use end to sew seam of same colour.

LEMON CUP CAKE:

With D instead of A, work as given for Chocolate cup cake to *.

Top:

Change to E. Beg with a k row, work 4 rows in st st.

Shape top:

1st row: (K4, k2tog) 6 times.
2nd row: (P3, p2tog) 6 times.
3rd row: (K2, k2tog) 6 times.
4th row: (P1, p2tog) 6 times.
5th row: (K2tog) 6 times. 6 sts.
6th and foll alt rows: P to end.
7th row: K into front and back of each st. 12 sts.
9th row: (K3, k into front and back of next st) 3 times.
11th row: (K4, k into front and back of next st) 3 times. 18 sts.
13th row: P to end.
15th row: (K4, k2tog) 3 times.
17th row: (K3, k2tog) 3 times.
19th row: (K2tog) 6 times.
Cut off yarn. Thread cut end through rem sts and draw up tightly.

CARROT CAKE:

Front and back: (Alike)

With F, cast on 20 sts.
Beg with a p row, cont in reverse st st and work 24 rows. Cast/bind off 3 sts at beg of next 2 rows and 2 sts at beg of foll 2 rows. Cast/bind off rem 10 sts.

Sides:

With F, cast on 56 sts.
1st row: (RS) K18, p1, k18, p1, k18.
2nd row: P18, k1, p18, k1, p18.
Rep last 2 rows twice more. Cast/bind off.

Top:

With C, cast on 20 sts.
Beg with a k row, work 6 rows in st st. Cast/bind off.

Icing/frosting:

With H instead of C, work as given for Top.

BIRTHDAY CAKE:

Base:

With E, cast on 19 sts. Beg with a k row, cont in st st, dec 1 st at each end of 4th and every foll 3rd row until 3 sts rem. Work 2 rows straight. P3tog and fasten off.

Sides:

With E, cast on 59 sts.
1st row: (RS) K9, p1, (k19, p1) twice, k9.

2nd row: P9, k1, (p19, k1) twice, p9.
Rep these 2 rows 3 times more, then work 1st row again with H and 2nd row again with G. Cont in E only, work 1st and 2nd rows 4 times more. Cast/bind off.

Top:

With C, cast on 19 sts.
Beg with a k row, cont in st st and work 2 rows.
Next row: (RS) K4 C, (mb with colour K, k4 C) 3 times. Cont in st st and C only, dec 1 st at each end of next and every foll 3rd row until 3 sts rem. Work 2 rows straight. P3tog and fasten off.

JAM SWISS ROLL:

With E, cast on 65 sts. Beg with a k row, work 3 rows in st st. Change to G and p 2 rows.
With E and beg with a p row, work 6 rows in st st. Change to G and p 2 rows.
With E and beg with a p row, work 3 rows in st st. Cast/bind off.

CHOCOLATE SWISS ROLL:

With B, cast on 65 sts. Beg with a k row, cont in st st. Work 3 rows B, 2 rows H, 6 rows B, 2 rows H and 3 rows B. Cast/bind off.

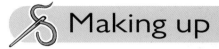 # Making up

CHOCOLATE CUP CAKE:

Join remainder of seam, leaving base open.
Turn RS out and stuff lightly with polyester toy filling.
Close opening in base.

Cherry bobble:

With G, cast on 3 sts.
K into front and back of each st. 6 sts.
Beg with a p row, work 5 rows in st st. K6tog and fasten off. Form into a small ball and sew to top of cake.

LEMON CUP CAKE:

Place small amount of toy filling into top of cake and then use mattress st to join side seam, using matching yarn colours and leaving base open. Stuff rest of cake lightly with toy filling and close opening in base. Secure a length of E to centre of cake base. Pass needle through cake and out at the top. Now take needle back down through cake and pull top down slightly to indent. Secure again to base of cake. Sew small glass bead to top of cake.

CARROT CAKE:

With scrap of I, embroider French knots randomly over Front and back to represent pieces of carrot. Sew row ends of top to row ends of side and sew in place around outer edges of Front and back, aligning p sts with lower corners and leaving a small gap in one seam. Stuff lightly and then sew opening closed. Sew Icing/frosting in place across top of cake.

BIRTHDAY CAKE:

Join row ends of Sides to form a circle. Placing this seam at centre back, sew Top in place with p sts at corners and point. Sew Base in place to match, leaving a small opening in seam. Stuff lightly and then sew opening closed.

JAM SWISS ROLL:

Cut a piece of lightweight polyester wadding/batting 2cm (¾in) wide x width of knitted strip. Place wadding/batting on WS of knitted strip between two contrast stripes. Fold cast-on and cast/bound-off edges over top so they meet in the middle and oversew seam. Carefully roll up strip, securing with small sts as you go. Sew end in place.

CHOCOLATE SWISS ROLL:

Work as given for Jam swiss roll.

Very thin scarf

Wear it wrapped or knotted and wound around your neck for a cool accessory to any outfit.

With ribbed ends and a long straight stretch of stocking/stockinette stitch, this ultra-thin scarf will wrap around your neck and still leave plenty to hang down as well.

GETTING STARTED

This is an easy pattern that is ideal for a beginner

Size:

Scarf is 8cm wide x 214cm long (3in x 84in)

How much yarn:

3 x 50g (2oz) balls of Rowan Wool Cotton DK, approx 113m (123 yards) per ball, in main colour A

1 ball in each of two contrast colours B and C

Needles:

Pair of 4mm (no. 8/US 6) knitting needles

Tension/gauge:

22 sts and 30 rows measures 10cm (4in) square over st st on 4mm (no. 8/US 6) needles

IT IS ESSENTIAL TO WORK TO THE STATED TENSION/ GAUGE TO ACHIEVE SUCCESS

What you have to do:

Work each end of scarf in double (k2, p2) rib. Continue four stitches at each side in rib, while main fabric is in stocking/stockinette stitch. Work stripes as instructed, joining in and cutting off colours as required. Cast/bind off in rib.

The Yarn

Rowan Wool Cotton DK is a blend of 50% wool and 50% cotton. Soft merino wool is mixed with cotton to create a versatile double knitting/light worsted weight yarn that is machine washable. There are plenty of fabulous colours to choose from for stripe combinations.

Abbreviations:

cm = centimetre(s);

cont = continue;

k = knit; **p** = purl;

rep = repeat;

RS = right side;

st(s) = stitch(es);

st st = stocking/
stockinette stitch

Note:

If possible, use a single
length of yarn for each
stripe to minimize ends.
Weave in ends neatly as
you work, or sew them in
afterwards, remembering
that front, back and edges
of scarf are visible
when worn.

Instructions

SCARF:

With A, cast on 22 sts.

1st row: (RS) K2, *p2, k2, rep from * to
end.

2nd row: P2, *k2, p2, rep from * to end.
Rep these 2 rows 11 times more.

Next row: (RS) K2, p2, k to last 4 sts, p2,
k2.

Next row: P2, k2, p to last 4 sts, k2,
p2.

Rep last 2 rows throughout, working in
colour sequence of 24 rows A, 6 rows B,
12 rows C, 6 rows B, 78 rows A, 6 rows
C, 78 rows A, 6 rows B, 78 rows A, 6
rows C, 78 rows A, 6 rows B, 78 rows A,
6 rows C, 78 rows A, 6 rows B, 12 rows
C, 6 rows B and 24 rows A.

Cont in A, work 24 rows in k2, p2 rib as
given for other end of scarf. Cast/bind off
in rib.

Making up

Press scarf to dimensions given using a
warm iron over a damp cloth.

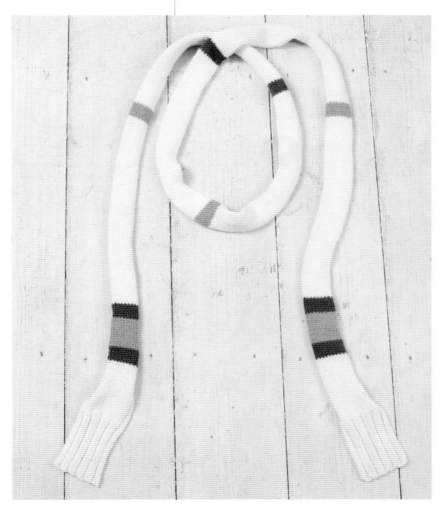

Index

Acknowledgements

Managing Editor: Clare Churly
Editors: Jane Ellis and Sarah Hoggett
Senior Art Editor: Juliette Norsworthy
Designer: Janis Utton
Production Controller: Sarah Kramer